ESCAPE
THE COMING
NIGHT

VOLUME 1

D1225790

Dr. David Jeremiah

Dr. Richard L. Plasket

with Dr. David Jeremiah

© 2001, 2005 by Turning Point for God
P.O. Box 3838
San Diego, CA 92163
All Rights Reserved

CONTENTS

About
Dr. David Jeremiah
and Turning Point

D r. David Jeremiah is the founder of Turning Point, a ministry committed to providing Christians with sound Bible teaching relevant to today's changing times through radio and television broadcasts, audio series, and books. Dr. Jeremiah's common-sense teaching on topics such as family, prayer, worship, angels, and biblical prophecy forms the foundation of Turning Point.

David and his wife, Donna, reside in El Cajon, California, where he is the senior pastor of Shadow Mountain Community Church and chancellor of San Diego Christian College. David and Donna have four children and six grandchildren.

In 1982, Dr. Jeremiah brought the same solid teaching to San Diego television that he shares weekly with his congregation. Shortly thereafter, Turning Point expanded its ministry to radio. Dr. Jeremiah's inspiring messages can now be heard worldwide on radio and television.

Because Dr. Jeremiah desires to know his listening audience, he travels nationwide holding "A Night of Encouragement" ministry rallies and Spiritual Enrichment conferences that touch the hearts and lives of many people. According to Dr. Jeremiah, "At some point in time, everyone reaches a turning point; and for every person, that moment is unique, an experience to hold onto forever. There's so much changing in today's world that sometimes it's difficult to choose the right path. Turning Point offers people an understanding of God's Word as well as the opportunity to make a difference in their lives."

Dr. Jeremiah has authored numerous books, including *Escape the Coming Night* (Revelation), *The Handwriting on the Wall* (Daniel), *Overcoming Loneliness, What the Bible Says About Angels, The Power of Encouragement, Prayer—The Great Adventure, God in You* (Holy Spirit), *Gifts from God* (Parenting), *Jesus' Final Warning, When Your World Falls Apart, Slaying the Giants in Your Life, My Heart's Desire, Sanctuary, The Things That Matter, Life Wide Open, The Prayer Matrix, Searching for Heaven on Earth,* and *The Secret of the Light.*

ABOUT THIS
STUDY GUIDE

The purpose of this Turning Point study guide is to reinforce Dr. David Jeremiah's dynamic, in-depth teaching in the Book of Revelation and to aid the reader in applying biblical truth to his or her daily life. This study guide is designed to be used in conjunction with Dr. Jeremiah's *Escape the Coming Night* audiocassette series, but it may be used by itself for personal or group Bible study.

STRUCTURE OF THE LESSONS

Each lesson is based on one of the tapes in the *Escape the Coming Night* audiocassette series and focuses on specific passages in the Bible. Each lesson is composed of the following elements:

- *Outline*

The outline at the beginning of the lesson gives a clear, concise picture of the passage being studied and provides a helpful framework for readers as they listen to Dr. Jeremiah's teaching.

- *Overview*

The overview summarizes Dr. Jeremiah's teaching on the passage being studied in the lesson. Readers should refer to the biblical passages in their own Bibles as they study the overview.

- *Application*

This section contains a variety of questions designed to help readers dig deeper into the lesson and the Scriptures and to apply the lesson to their daily lives. For Bible study groups or Sunday school classes, these questions will provide a springboard for group discussion and interaction.

- *Did You Know?*

This section presents a fascinating fact, historical note, or insight that adds a point of interest to the preceding lesson.

USING THIS GUIDE FOR GROUP STUDY

The lessons in this study guide are suitable for Sunday school classes, small-group studies, elective Bible studies, or home Bible study groups. Each person in the group should have his or her own study guide.

When possible, the study guide should be used with the corresponding tape series. You may wish to assign the study guide as homework prior to the meeting of the group and then use the meeting time to listen to the tape and discuss the lesson.

FOR CONTINUING STUDY

A complete catalog of Dr. Jeremiah's materials for personal and group study is available through Turning Point. To obtain a catalog, additional study guides, or more information about Turning Point, call 1-800-947-1993 or write to: Turning Point, P.O. Box 3838, San Diego, CA 92163.

Dr. Jeremiah's *Turning Point* radio broadcast is currently heard on more than 1000 national and international radio outlets. Contact Turning Point for radio and television program times and stations in your area.

ESCAPE THE COMING NIGHT
VOLUME I

INTRODUCTION

Take a poll among Christians who read their Bibles faithfully, and I can guarantee at least one consistent result: Very few Christians, even those who believe "all Scripture is given by inspiration of God, and is profitable . . ." (2 Timothy 3:16), spend much time reading or studying the Book of Revelation. And here's another result I can guarantee: If you take a poll among the pastors of those same Christians, very few of them have spent much time studying Revelation either, and hardly any of them have ever preached an in-depth series of messages from its text.

Why is that? Bible-believing Christians certainly affirm that Revelation is part of the "all Scripture . . ." referred to above. If all Scripture is profitable for us, why do we ignore one of the largest books in the Bible?

As a pastor, I am well aware of the reasons Christians avoid Revelation. "It's too complicated." "I can't understand what it's talking about." "It has to do with prophecy. How do I know what to believe?" I would not argue with anyone who has been discouraged by reading Revelation. It certainly is more challenging than reading narrative history such as is found in the books of Genesis, Chronicles, and Acts. Those books read almost like historical novels which modern readers enjoy. Even the four Gospels read like biographies, and Paul's epistles are letters that contain a train of thought that is not difficult to follow. We would agree with Peter who found some of Paul's letters "hard to understand" (2 Peter 3:16), but at least they read like "plain English" to us. Revelation seems to be in a different category altogether. And indeed it is, but it is a category that is "profitable for . . ." our spiritual lives.

Revelation is a form of biblical literature called "apocalyptic," meaning it uses symbols and imagery to reveal the secret purposes of God for the present and future ("apocalypse" means "revelation").

Interestingly, apocalyptic literature was common and understandable at the time the Apostle John wrote Revelation because its roots are in the prophecies of the Old Testament. If we have a difficult time understanding the Book of Revelation today, it is first and foremost because of our lack of familiarity with the Old Testament.

John recorded the revelation he received from God and sent it to the churches in Asia Minor near the end of the first century A.D. Its purpose was to correlate with what God had already revealed in the Old Testament and what the apostles had written in the epistles about the future from God's perspective. Revelation is eminently understandable when we approach it from the perspective that it was written to be read and applied. It was written to lift up the sovereignty and majesty of God, to encourage the end-time Church, and to lay out the broad (and often very detailed) parameters of God's plan for the future of the Church, the unsaved, and planet earth. Doesn't that sound like a book worth reading? Besides, it's the only book of the Bible that promises a blessing for studying it!

Happily, Revelation divides itself into three sections (Revelation 1:19). In this first of four study guides, we will complete sections one and two which cover Revelation, chapters 1-4. In these introductory chapters you will meet the One who gave the revelation to John, and you will get to know seven historical churches which provide a sweeping panorama of the 2,000 years of Christian church history—all in four chapters of the Bible!

God gave Revelation to you. If you'll dip your toes in the water in this first volume, the next time a survey is taken about favorite books of the Bible, I can guarantee Revelation will be one of yours.

A PANORAMA OF PROPHECY

Selected Scriptures

In this lesson we gain an overview of the subject of biblical prophecy.

You will find more in-depth information on this lesson in the book *Escape the Coming Night,* chapters 1 and 2.

OUTLINE

Some people believe that death is the final certainty of life. But there is one thing even more certain than death—the return of Christ. Those believers who are alive the day Christ returns will never die. Nothing in this life is more certain than the return of Jesus Christ.

I. **Jesus Must Come Back**
   A. He Must Come Back To Take His Church To Be with Him
   B. He Must Come Back To Judge the World
   C. He Must Come Back To Rule the World

II. **What Is Going To Happen When Jesus Comes Back?**
   A. The Tribulation
   B. The Man of Sin (the Antichrist)
   C. The Millennium

III. **How Prophecy Should Impact the Christian's Life**

For God, everything is "now." There is no past, present, or future with God, for He sees all things from the beginning to the end at once. As a result, the future is not an "unknown" for God as it is for us. Everything for God is in the "present tense"—including the future.

But because the Bible is a book written in human terms, much of its content has to do with that which has not yet come to pass as far as time is concerned. In fact, at least one-fifth of the Bible addressed matters of the future at the time it was written. Many of the Bible's predictions have already come to pass, such as those relating to the birth, death, and resurrection of Jesus Christ. Yet many more prophecies remain unfulfilled, especially those having to do with events surrounding the Second Coming of Christ. For instance, the return of Christ to earth is referred to 318 times in the New Testament, far more times than the number of chapters of Scripture in the New Testament. It is referred to in the Old Testament many times as well.

The book we will study in this series, Revelation, has to do almost exclusively with end-time events associated with the return of Christ. Two angels told the disciples of Christ that He would return to earth in the manner in which they had seen Him ascend into heaven (Acts 1:11). That simple, yet profound, statement forms the bedrock of the hope of the Church—the glorious appearing of her Savior and Lord a second time. Christ Himself is the center of all prophecy concerning His return, as the first line of Revelation indicates: "The Revelation of Jesus Christ . . ." (Revelation 1:1). "Revelation" means "unfolding" or "unveiling." The Book of Revelation, then, is the unveiling of Jesus Christ at the end of time.

JESUS MUST COME BACK

It is important in the initial state of our consideration of Revelation to ask, "Why must Christ return to earth?"

He Must Come Back To Take His Church To Be with Him

The Church is presented in 2 Corinthians, Ephesians, and Revelation as the Bride of Christ. As a bride eagerly awaits the day of her marriage to the bridegroom, so the Church eagerly awaits the appearing of her bridegroom, Christ. The first thing that happens when Christ returns is He takes the Church to heaven to enjoy the marriage supper of the Lamb, the symbolic uniting of Christ and His bride to be one forever in eternity.

In addition to the revelry of the marriage supper there will also be the judgment seat of Christ. After the Rapture of the Church, while the Tribulation is taking place on earth, the Church is being judged in heaven. The works we have done, and their continuing influence on the lives of others, will be the basis of that judgment. Rewards will be given for faithfulness to Christ, and loss will be suffered for lack of faithfulness. This judgment is not to determine whether we go to heaven—indeed, we are already there when it takes place. It is an evaluation of our work for Christ on earth.

First Thessalonians, chapter four, details several things which will happen when Christ returns for His Church at the Rapture. From many places in Scripture, Matthew 24, for instance, we draw insights as to the signs that will precede His coming. And I personally believe we are beginning to see many of those signs appear today. Nothing is left which must take place before Christ returns for His Bride. He could come today—He could come at any time.

He Must Come Back To Judge the World

Christ comes twice—first, in the air to gather His Bride, the Church, to Himself. Second, seven years later, He comes to earth to judge the world. He will come to take "vengeance on those who do not know God," punishing them with "everlasting destruction" (2 Thessalonians 1:8-9). He will judge both "the living and the dead at His appearing" (2 Timothy 4:1). The return of Christ as judge is strong motivation for the living to bring their lives in step with the Gospel and live for Christ.

He Must Come Back To Rule the World

Daniel 7:13-14 tells us of the ultimate rule which Christ will assume when He returns the second time. The focus in the passage is on the dominion given to Christ, rulership over all "peoples, nations, and languages." This period is called the Millennium, the thousand year reign of Christ, and it follows the Tribulation, beginning after the judgment of Christ at His Second Coming to earth. The One who

The Bible instructs us to always be looking for the day of Christ's return . . . with sober and Spirit-led discernment. How can we "see the Day approaching" if we aren't even looking for it? We are to investigate what the Bible has to say and ask God to help us. God intends knowledge of future events to help us "occupy" with a sense of urgency until the Lord returns.

David Jeremiah
Hearing the Master's Voice

never ruled even His own tiny country of Israel is going to one day return to rule the entire earth. The Apostle John writes that "the kingdoms of this world have become the kingdoms of our Lord and of His Christ" (Revelation 11:15).

WHAT IS GOING TO HAPPEN WHEN JESUS COMES BACK?

Matthew 24 begins with questions to Jesus from His disciples about the nature of the end times, the signs leading up to His coming again. People have pondered these questions ever since. The answers He gave them point not to the Rapture of the church but to the establishment of His kingdom on earth. Because the Rapture precedes the kingdom, those signs apply generally, but not specifically, to that event. In fact, the Rapture is like a trigger that sets in motion many events which will take place on earth immediately prior to Christ's Second Coming.

The Tribulation

When the Church leaves the earth at the Rapture, so also the Holy Spirit departs. That means there is no restraining influence of righteousness on earth. Man, without any restraining moral or spiritual influence, will create a terrible situation on earth known as the Tribulation. Revelation 11-18 deals with the events of this seven-year time period, a period of conflict, confusion, and wickedness. Believers are not destined for the Tribulation period. The Rapture of the Church is "pre-tribulational;" it happens before the Tribulation begins. The Church will be kept from the "hour of trial which shall come upon the whole world" (Revelation 3:10).

There are three primary characteristics of the Tribulation period:

1. Worldwide judgment

   This is revealed in the Book of Revelation through symbols such as seals, trumpets, and vials from which judgment comes upon the whole world.

2. Persecution of Israel

   In the Old Testament the Tribulation is called "the time of Jacob's trouble" (Jeremiah 30:7). The Jewish people will suffer intense persecution during this period.

3. Salvation of multitudes

   Those who did not hear the Gospel prior to the Rapture will have opportunity to do so during the Tribulation, and many will believe. Second Thessalonians 2:10-12 says a strong delusion will come upon those who heard, but did not believe, the Gospel prior to the Rapture. Those will not get a second chance. But many who have not heard the Gospel before will hear it and believe, and many will be martyred for their faith.

The Man of Sin (the Antichrist)

During the Tribulation, the "Man of Sin," the Antichrist, will be the dominant person in the world. All of the evil of Satan himself will be incarnate in this man. He is represented in Scripture as a "lawless one" (2 Thessalonians 2:9) and as a beast (Revelation 13:1-18). Both are appropriate designations for his character and his actions during the Tribulation. Just when it seems the Antichrist has caused there to be no more hope for the world, Christ will appear and end the Tribulation on earth with the Battle of Armageddon.

The Millennium

"Millennium" means "thousand years," and it derives from Revelation 20:1-6 which describes the rule and reign of Christ on earth. For a thousand years Christ will rule as king over all the earth from His capitol, Jerusalem. The saints of God, who returned with Him for the Battle of Armageddon, rule with Christ during the Millennium. We rule from the New Jerusalem which is located above the earth, and help to oversee a thousand years of peace and righteousness on earth. Satan will be bound during that period so that peace may flourish and the knowledge of the Lord may fill the earth. Everyone entering the Millennium will be a believer, having believed in Christ during the Tribulation (the wicked will have been judged at this point). But children will be born who populate the earth during the Millennium, some of whom rebel against the righteous rule of Christ. Satan is loosed for a time at the end of the Millennium and stirs up a final rebellion on earth among those who haven't believed during the thousand years. The final judgment of the world, the Great White Throne Judgment, concludes the Millennium and ushers in eternity.

HOW PROPHECY SHOULD IMPACT THE CHRISTIAN'S LIFE

Prophecy is a fascinating part of Scripture, but if we study it simply as a mental exercise we are missing the point. A number of key Scriptures reveal the impact prophecy should have on our life:

1. 1 Corinthians 4:5. The prospect of a future judgment by Christ should keep us from passing judgment on one another now. We should spend our time in God's work, not in evaluating others.

2. 1 Corinthians 11:26. We proclaim the Lord's death "till He comes" whenever we participate in the Lord's Supper. That communion meal is a reminder that we are awaiting the com-

ing again of the One who died for us. The Lord's Supper is a rehearsal for the Marriage Supper of the Lamb.

3. Colossians 3:1-4. If we understand the future and the coming again of Christ we will respond to life spiritually. We will set our affection on things above because we know that is where Christ is and from where He will come to receive us to Himself.

4. 1 Thessalonians 3:12-13. If we are to stand blameless before Him at His return we must relate to one another in love during His absence. Our personal relationships are affected by a proper understanding of prophecy.

5. 2 Timothy 4:1-2. Written to pastors, these verses exhort us to preach the Word and do the ministry God has given in light of the return of Christ, at which time an account will have to be given. The return of Christ affects our ministry.

6. Hebrews 10:25. The closer we get to the day of Christ's appearing, the closer we should be drawing ourselves together with other believers. As the clouds darken in this world in the last days, every believer will need the encouragement of the church to remain strong.

7. James 5:7-8. Living in light of the Lord's return should bring patience, and therefore stability, to all we do. As a farmer learns to wait patiently for his seed to bear fruit, so we wait patiently for the final harvest of God.

8. 1 John 3:2-3. Everyone who has the hope of Christ's return will purify himself in anticipation of that event. Would you want Christ to appear at the moment you were in the midst of unholy behavior? The expectation of His return should purify our lives.

> *At 17 my parents went on a trip and left me to take care of things at home. I let dishes, laundry, etc. pile up. I didn't know exactly when they were coming back, but it would be within a three-day window. At the beginning of the three days, I cleaned up everything because I wanted to be ready when my parents returned. How do we prepare for the Lord's return?*
>
> *We stay ready, so we never have to scramble around to get ready. We should live our lives as the book of Titus tells us—in a godly, righteous way, so that we might always be ready.*
>
> David Jeremiah
> **Hearing the Master's Voice**

9. Jude 20-23. If we believe Christ is coming back, we will do everything we can to reach the lost for Christ, to pull them out of the fire. Every day that passes is one less day we have to reach an unsaved person for Christ.

10. 1 Thessalonians 4:16-18. Perhaps the greatest impact of all on our lives is freedom from the fear of death. When Christ returns for His Church the first ones to meet Him will be "the dead in Christ." Whether we are living or dead at the moment of Christ's return makes no difference to the believer, for all who are alive or dead in Him will rise to meet Him in the air—"and thus we shall always be with the Lord. Therefore comfort one another with these words."

As we study the Revelation of Christ, may the blessed hope of His return be of great comfort to you as you wait for Him.

APPLICATION

1. Read Acts 1:6-11.

   a. What were the disciples most focused on following Christ's resurrection? (verse 6)

   b. What was Jesus' basic response to their questions about "future things"? (verse 7)

   c. Instead of giving them detailed knowledge about the future, what did He give them? (verse 8)

   d. What happened next? Given their stares into heaven, how surprised do you think the disciples were at His departure? (verse 9)

   e. What assurance were they given by the two men who appeared? (verse 11)

   f. Given the fixed scope of their assignment, how long do you think they anticipated Jesus' absence might be?

   g. How would you interpret Matthew 24:14 with Acts 1:8?

2. Record your own insights about the impact the return of Christ should have on the Church from the 10 passages mentioned briefly in the lesson.

   a. 1 Corinthians 4:5

b. 1 Corinthians 11:26

c. Colossians 3:1-4

d. 1 Thessalonians 3:12-13

e. 2 Timothy 4:1-2

f. Hebrews 10:25

g. James 5:7-8

h. 1 John 3:2-3

i. Jude 20-23

j. 1 Thessalonians 4:16-18

SPEAKING OF THE FUTURE . . .

In 1831, a church-going Vermont farmer named William Miller began sharing with his friends a conviction he had guarded for several years: Jesus would return between March 21, 1843, and March 21, 1844. When Jesus failed to appear, Miller recalculated and set the date at October 22, 1844. Hundreds of his followers sold their homes and quit their jobs, only to become angry when Miller's predictions failed to come true.

This story illustrates how focused some believers are on the future. Their lives are so centered on what will be, they ignore what they could be doing for Christ in the here and now.

While it's important to know and understand what will happen in the future according to biblical prophecy, we must be careful not to neglect today. In other words, we are not to be so heavenly minded that we are no earthly good.

Where do you stand on prophecy? Are you so concerned with the future that you miss out on the opportunities of today? Or are you so settled into what is that you have not considered what will be? All Scripture is inspired by God, including the prophetic parts. Prophecy can enrich the way you live today as you view the present in light of God's plan for the future.

TAKE HEED THAT NO ONE DECEIVES YOU.

—Jesus in Matthew 24:4

GETTING EXCITED ABOUT REVELATION

Selected Scriptures

In this lesson we discover what is unique about the Book of Revelation.

You will find more in-depth information on this lesson in the book *Escape the Coming Night,* chapters 1 and 2.

OUTLINE

Most people who are confused by the Book of Revelation have never read it, much less studied it in a disciplined fashion. Revelation was meant to be understood and promises blessings to those who take the time to mine its riches. It is a book of victory for the victorious.

    I. **Revelation Is a Misunderstood Book**

    II. **Revelation Is a Messianic Book**

    III. **Revelation Is a Mysterious Book**

    IV. **Revelation Is a Meaningful Book**
        A. The Spirit of God Opened the Book for Us To Read
        B. The Spirit of God Outlined the Book
        C. The Spirit of God Operates Within the Book

    V. **Revelation Is a Miraculous Book**

    VI. **Revelation Is a Motivational Book**

    VII. **Revelation Is a Majestic Book**

  VIII. **Revelation Is the Maximal Book**

    IX. **Revelation Is a Militant Book**

W hen Mt. Saint Helens erupted in Oregon in 1980, a
number of people perished who refused to heed the
warnings of impending danger. They had lived safely
near the mountain for years and refused to believe that what they
considered a friend would bring harm to them. Unfortunately they
were wrong. There are many more than the few who died near Mt.
Saint Helens who are ignoring similar warning signs today, warnings
of the end of the age. The Book of Revelation predicts with startling
detail events which are destined to unfold upon planet earth, events
leading to the climax of the world as we know it. And yet few are
reading and heeding the warning signs so plainly set before us.

Before beginning the verse-by-verse study of Revelation which
commences in the next lesson, it will help us to have an overview
of the book as a whole. The best way to do that is list and examine
some of the characteristics of Revelation, that which makes it unique
among the books of the New Testament.

REVELATION IS A
MISUNDERSTOOD BOOK

Six attitudes prevail concerning the Book of Revelation.

1. Some people are uninformed. They have no interest in the
   Bible, let alone the Book of Revelation. They know nothing
   about the book and have little interest in it beyond the realm
   of curiosity.

2. Some are unbelieving. They are spiritually undiscerning.
   When the natural man picks up a book like Revelation and
   tries to read and understand it, there is no spiritual compre-
   hension because "the natural man does not receive the things
   of the Spirit of God" (1 Corinthians 2:14).

3. Some are uninterested. These may be found in the church
   among the converted. They are "not into prophecy." They say,
   "Don't tell me about Revelation. Give me something practical
   that will help me with my life."

4. Some are unfriendly. These are supposed Christians who
   believe that the book is a compilation of heathen mythologies,
   fables, fancies and folklore. They do not accept the Book of
   Revelation at face value in its literal interpretation.

5. Some are untaught. These are the people within the church
   who are interested in the book but have never been taught the
   meaning of it. I am shocked at the number of people outside
   of my own church who tell me they have never in their entire

Christian experience received any systematic teaching on the Book of Revelation.

6. Some are understanding. Since you are reading this study guide on Revelation, I trust this is the group you are in—those who want to learn to understand and apply the spiritual riches waiting to be discovered in the Book of Revelation.

REVELATION IS A MESSIANIC BOOK

By that I mean it is a book about the Messiah, a book about Jesus Christ. No less a Bible scholar than Martin Luther, the father of the Protestant Reformation, went to his grave thinking little of the Book of Revelation. His opinion was based on the fact that, to him, the book contained little about Jesus Christ. Actually nothing could be further from the truth. Revelation is "the Revelation of Jesus Christ" (Revelation 1:1). Unfortunately, in some early editions of English Bibles, Revelation was titled "The Revelation of St. John the Divine," referring to the Apostle John who wrote down the content of the book. But that is erroneous—the titles of Bible books in our English Bibles are not part of the inspired text.

The four Gospels present Christ in His earthly life and ministry, and His death and resurrection—the humiliation of Christ. And the epistles give only glimpses of His glory in passages such as Philippians 2, where Paul says every knee will bow to Christ as king one day. But Revelation reverses the humiliation of Christ seen in the rest of the New Testament and reveals Him in all of His glory as King of Kings and Lord of Lords. In Revelation we see Christ assume His rightful place as ruler over all the earth. Revelation is preeminently a book about Jesus Christ, the Messiah.

Many people treat the Book of Revelation like the priest and Levite treated the man who was beaten and robbed in the story of the Good Samaritan . . . they pass by on the other side. The devil has turned thousands of people away from this portion of God's Word. He does not want anyone to read a book that tells of his being cast out of heaven . . . Nor is he anxious for us to read of the ultimate triumph of his number one enemy, Jesus Christ. The more you study the Book of Revelation, the more you understand why Satan fights so hard to keep God's people away from it.

Louis Talbot

REVELATION IS A MYSTERIOUS BOOK

Symbols occur throughout Scripture as a vehicle for divine revelation, but this book of the New Testament contains more symbols than any other Bible book. The book is filled with mystery. It portrays things seen and unseen. It portrays things in the body and out of the body. It portrays things of the world and things of the world to come. It symbolically portrays angels and demons and principalities in the heavenlies. It speaks of agents and of nations and of potentates, and sometimes the symbols represent people. In the first chapter, we are introduced to Jesus as a judge with a two-edged sword coming out of His mouth (verse 16).

There were three primary reasons for the heavy use of symbolism in the Book of Revelation.

1. Symbolism is not weakened by time. The symbols live from century to century and never lose their meaning.

2. Symbols impart values and arouse emotions. Which is stronger—to call a man a dictator or call him a beast? Which is more graphic—discussing the "world system" or "Babylon the Great?" Symbols arouse emotion and hold interest.

3. Symbols functioned as a kind of spiritual code. John wrote while in exile on the island of Patmos. The Roman Empire under Emperor Domitian was mounting an all-out campaign against the Christian church. The last apostle, John, responded to that campaign with a book which could not be interpreted by Roman authorities. It drew so heavily on Jewish apocalyptic imagery from the Old Testament that no one but informed Bible readers could understand it.

By the time we finish our study of Revelation we will understand all the "mysterious" symbols in the book.

REVELATION IS A MEANINGFUL BOOK

There are three reasons why Revelation is such a meaningful book.

> *The escape route has been mapped out for almost two thousand years. . . . Many people think time is growing short before Christ returns. In the past twenty years, since Bible prophecy captured the attention of the "Jesus" generation, history has been in high gear. Are we listening today to the warnings from the mountain of evidence in front of us?*
>
> *David Jeremiah*
> ***Escape the Coming Night***

The Spirit of God Opened the Book for Us To Read (Revelation 22:10)

Jesus tells John at the end of the revelation he has recorded not to seal up the words of the prophecy he has seen and written down, "for the time is at hand." In other words, the revelation was given by Christ to John for the church to read. (Compare this to Daniel 12:4 where Daniel was told to do the opposite: Seal up the words of his book until the end times.) Revelation, as we shall see, was addressed directly to seven churches who were being persecuted, but the Church of all ages needs that same message.

The Spirit of God Outlined the Book (1:19)

The outline of the Book of Revelation is given right in the book: "Write the things which you have seen, and the things which are, and the things which will take place after this" (1:19). That simple sentence forms a workable outline of the whole book.

I. The things which you have seen: Chapter 1 (God in Glory)

II. The things which are: Chapters 2-3 (The Church on Earth)

III. The things which will take place after this: Chapters 4-22 (The Government of the Future)

The Spirit of God Operates Within the Book

Unlike other Bible books, Revelation often interprets itself, giving the meaning of many of the symbols it employs (e.g., 1:16 and 1:20; 1:13 and 1:20; 4:5; 5:6; 5:8; 9:1 and 9:11; 12:4 and 12:9; 17:1 and 17:15; 19:8). The Holy Spirit gave the interpretation right in the text in many places in the book.

REVELATION IS A MIRACULOUS BOOK

The reason it is miraculous is because it tells the future before it happens. It writes history before history is accomplished. It is the only prophetic book in the New Testament, and God intended for it to be read that way, as a book that reveals the future (22:7, 20, 17-19). Some people interpret the Book of Revelation as a book of church history written in symbolic language, but that is wrong. It is a book about the future.

REVELATION IS A MOTIVATIONAL BOOK

This is the only book in the Bible that motivates its readers by promising a blessing for those who will read and obey it. The promise is made both at the beginning and at the end of the book (1:3 and 22:7). When God tells me plainly there is a way I can be blessed, especially so simple a way as reading and obeying part of the Bible, I'm motivated to do it. I want to be blessed! There are seven distinct beatitudes, or blessings, recorded in the Book of Revelation: 1:3; 14:13; 16:15; 19:9; 20:6; 22:7, 14. If you want God's blessing in your life, here is a God-ordained way to get it: Read and apply the message of the Book of Revelation. Why would you turn down an offer to be blessed such as that?

REVELATION IS A MAJESTIC BOOK

Revelation is the book of the throne, the book where we see Christ in all of His majesty. In fact, the word "throne" appears in the book 46 times. The word "king" is found 37 times, and the words "power and authority" are found 40 times. Here in the Book of Revelation God is presented in glory and in majesty. Nothing reveals the majesty of the book like the reaction of John to the personal revelation of Jesus Christ as it is recorded in Revelation 1:17. When John the apostle saw a vision of the majesty of Christ he "fell at His feet as dead." That was John's response to the view of God in His glory and all of His majesty. That is not an uncommon response to the glory of God, for the same thing happened to Daniel in the Old Testament (Daniel 10:7-9). When we see God in all of His glory as John and Daniel saw Him, we will cease being as flippant about God as we often are. We, too, will be on our face as though we were dead.

REVELATION IS THE MAXIMAL BOOK

Revelation is the book of completion and consummation.

In Genesis you have the commencement of Heaven and earth.
In Revelation you have the consummation of Heaven and earth.

In Genesis you have the entrance of sin and the curse.
In Revelation you have the end of sin and the curse.

In Genesis you have the dawn of Satan and his activities.
In Revelation you have the doom of Satan and his activities.

In Genesis you have the tree of life relinquished.
In Revelation you have the tree of life regained.

In Genesis death makes its entrance.
In Revelation death makes its exit.

In Genesis sorrow begins.
In Revelation sorrow is banished.

Revelation is the terminus of everything that happens throughout the whole Bible. All of the small threads and themes that run throughout Scripture find their culmination in Revelation. Like railroad tracks which come from all over the country and meet at a Grand Central Station of biblical themes . . . Revelation is that terminal.

REVELATION IS A MILITANT BOOK

The major message of the Book of Revelation is the glorious victory of Jesus Christ over all of His enemies. Those who identify with the Lord are called "overcomers," and there are eight promises given to them: 2:7, 11, 17, 26; 3:5, 12, 21; 21:7. One verse about overcomers is the key verse of them all: "And they overcame him by the blood of the Lamb and by the word of their testimony, and they did not love their lives to the death" (12:11). In context in the book this verse describes how martyrs for the cause of Christ won a battle against the forces of evil which were arrayed against God. There are three ways in which these martyrs overcame the power of the enemy.

1. By the blood of the Lamb

   You can't be an overcomer if your sins haven't been washed clean by the shed blood of Christ. You must be born again in Christ to be an overcomer.

2. By the word of their testimony

   This refers to spoken, verbal testimony. The people who I know who are overcomers are those who are fearlessly telling others about Christ as a part of their daily life.

3. By not loving their lives unto the death

   You can't be an overcomer if you are focused on preserving and enhancing your life in this world.

Revelation is a book for present and future overcomers. May God give us grace to make the future victory of God our reality today.

APPLICATION

1. From each of the following Scriptures, explain how Revelation gives the interpretation for some of its own symbolism.

   a. 1:16 and 1:20

   b. 1:13 and 1:20

   c. 4:5

   d. 5:6

   e. 5:8

   f. 9:1 and 9:11

   g. 12:4 and 12:9

   h. 17:1 and 17:15

   i. 19:8

2. Identify the blessings promised to those who heed the prophecy of Revelation.

   a. 1:3

   b. 14:13

c. 16:15

d. 19:9

e. 20:6

f. 22:7

g. 22:14

3. Evaluate yourself on the three characteristics of an overcomer as found in Revelation 12:11.

   a. "the blood of the Lamb"

   b. "the word of their testimony"

   c. "loved not their lives unto death"

Do you ever feel like you are far away from God?

John, the beloved apostle of Jesus Christ, though exiled to a barren island in the Aegean Sea, was not exiled from God. God, the Living One, went with him. For John, being shut away from the world on a prison island, meant being alone with God. While on Patmos, John received a magnificent revelation of earth's and mankind's future.

Across the centuries, God has walked with people of faith in dark circumstances. An innocent Joseph sat in a prison. Rizpah spent months guarding the dead bodies of her sons. Martin Luther walked through deep depression. In each case, the living God walked with them through these dark circumstances. These people came through their bend in the road because God was with them every step of the way.

God uses the difficult times in our lives to show us amazing things. You may experience isolation on every side, but you can walk in confidence. As God was with John on Patmos, He is with you. God won't desert you. You can trust Him fully through every difficult experience. You will never be exiled from God.

I AM WITH YOU ALWAYS, EVEN TO THE END OF THE AGE.

—Jesus in Matthew 28:20

THE INSIDE COVER OF THE BOOK

Revelation 1:1-8

In this lesson we discover how we received the Book of Revelation.

You will find more in-depth information on this lesson in the book *Escape the Coming Night*, chapters 1 and 2.

OUTLINE

In a few moments in the aisle of a bookstore we can collect all the pertinent information that leads to a buying decision—or not—for a book that interests us. The first few verses of Revelation reveal the same things: the author, publisher, and purpose of the book.

   I.   **The Preface to the Book**
      A. It Is a Prophetic Book
      B. It Is a Pictorial Book
      C. It Is a Profitable Book

  II.   **The People Addressed in the Book**

 III.   **The Publisher of the Book**
      A. From God the Father
      B. From God the Spirit
      C. From God the Son

  IV.   **The Personal Dedication of the Book**
      A. Who Loved Us
      B. Who Loosed Us
      C. Who Lifted Us

   V.   **The Purpose of the Book**
      A. The Presentation of the King
      B. The Program of the Kingdom

L ike most preachers and teachers, I enjoy books. I collect them, I review them, I read them, I examine them, and I have even written a few of my own. I even appreciate the craft of bookmaking and book publishing—how books are put together, how the story they tell is laid out. Books in our modern day follow a fairly predictable pattern on the outside as well as the inside. Components of a book are consistently the same: the title, a preface, an indication of whom the book is written for, perhaps an introduction, the name of the publisher, a dedication page, and so on. Interestingly, most of those same components can be found in ancient books as well, including the Book of Revelation.

In the first eight verses of Revelation we find the information that you would normally find informing you about a book published in our day, information to help you get excited about reading and enjoying the book. So in this lesson we'll get an introduction to the book as a whole by studying the first eight verses and discovering the preface, the people addressed, the publisher, the personal dedication, and the purpose of Revelation.

THE PREFACE TO THE BOOK (1:1-3)

"Preface" means "to say before." Therefore, the preface of a book contains the comments made by the author before getting into the book's contents.

It Is a Prophetic Book (1:1)

The word "revelation" comes from the Greek word *apokalupsis*, or "apocalypse." When we hear the word "apocalypse" we think of horrible and frightening disasters associated with the end of the world. But Hollywood's definition of the word is different from the Bible's. In Greek, the word "apocalypse" simply means "an uncovering, unveiling, setting forth, or manifestation of." Therefore, the "apocalypse of Jesus Christ" is the "uncovering or making known of Jesus Christ." The primary focus of the Book of Revelation is not to paint a picture of the end times, though it does help us do that. It is primarily to unveil the Lord Jesus Christ in His role as coming King over all the earth.

The preface continues in verse one to say the book will reveal "things which must shortly take place." The word translated "shortly" is from *tachos*, from which we get our word "tachometer"— the gauge which measures revolutions per minute (R.P.M.) of an engine. In the Greek it refers to something which will happen suddenly or quickly. It doesn't mean quickly as in "tomorrow"—but quickly as in a succession of events once they begin to unfold.

It Is a Pictorial Book (1:2)

Three or four times in Revelation we are told that these are the things which we are to be shown, a demonstration. This is not just a book that is written in words but in pictures as well. It is a visible book that demonstrates in symbols and in images what's going to happen in the future. The author John is writing about things "he saw." The images and pictures God showed John on the Island of Patmos are the images he describes for us in Revelation. Notice the chain of communication of these images. Verse one says the Father gave the message to the Son, and the Son sent it to John by way of an angel.

It Is a Profitable Book (1:3)

In our last lesson we noted the many different blessings promised to the reader of the Book of Revelation, and verse three contains the first of those promises. Verse three contains four ways in which Revelation is profitable for us.

1. It is profitable for personal application.

   Revelation is a book the devil hates. It tells of his ultimate doom and the ultimate victory of the Lord Jesus Christ. He does not want anyone to read the Book of Revelation. If I heard from God that by reading the Book of Revelation I could be blessed, I believe I would read it. I'd read it out loud. I'd read it as often as I could. It is the only book in all of the Bible that has its own special blessing promised for reading and obeying it.

2. It is profitable for public assembly.

   The Book of Revelation is profitable not only for reading but for hearing. It is sad that we don't read the Scriptures aloud in our churches much these days, for that was apparently the practice of the early church. Justyn Martyr, a leader in the early church (ca. A.D. 140) said that "the memoirs of the Apostles were read in the local assembly," referring obviously to their epistles. Public reading may also be what Paul referred to when he told Timothy to "give attention to reading" (1 Timothy 4:13).

One of my friends has an eight-foot bookshelf filled with current motivational best-sellers. I asked him if he had ever considered one of the greatest motivational treatises in the world, the Book of Revelation. He probably thought I had flipped out, but I hope he reads this book.

David Jeremiah
Escape the Coming Night

3. It is profitable for practical admonition.

Those are blessed who "keep the things which are written in it." The book is not only to be read and heard, but to be obeyed. A phrase repeated often in Revelation is, "He who has an ear, let him hear . . ." (e.g., 2:7, 11, 29; 3:6, 13, 22; 13:9). It's similar to what we mean when we say, "If the shoe fits, wear it." John means to say that if what you are reading applies to you, then you need to obey it and appropriate it for your life.

4. It is profitable for prophetic anticipation (1:3).

John says "the time is near." It's like the small boy who heard, for the first time, the family clock chime all the way to 12 and exclaimed to his mother, "Mom, it's later than it's ever been!" That's the message of Revelation—it was later than it had ever been when John wrote the book, and it is later than it has ever been now. People get caught up in trying to set a date for the return of Christ, but that is futile. All we need to know is that it "is near"—meaning nothing else has to happen on the prophetic calendar before Christ returns.

We will move quickly now through the rest of the information about the Book of Revelation presented by John.

THE PEOPLE ADDRESSED IN THE BOOK (1:4A)

While the Apostle Paul wrote separate letters to seven different churches, the Apostle John wrote one letter and sent it to seven churches. The entire Book of Revelation was sent to seven churches in Asia (they are listed in verse 11). Once again we find the number "seven"—the number of completeness—which is so prominent throughout Scripture. Looking at a map, you will notice these seven churches take the shape of a rough circle. These churches were representative of all the churches of John's day.

THE PUBLISHER OF THE BOOK (1:4-8)

The name of the publishing house today might be "Triune Publishers" since Revelation was published by the Father, Son, and Spirit of God.

From God the Father

God is Him who is and who was and who will be (verse 4), the "I am" of Exodus 3:13-14 who introduced Himself to Moses at the burning bush. We know this is the Father since the Son is mentioned separately in verse 5.

From God the Spirit

The "seven Spirits" before God's throne (verse 4) refer to the fullness, or completeness, of the Holy Spirit. In Isaiah 11:1-2 we find seven characteristics of the Spirit of God listed. We think of the Spirit as one, which He is, but He is also manifold in the manifestations of His character.

From God the Son

Christ is "the faithful witness" of verse 5 and the final publisher of the revelation John received. Throughout the book John ascribes title after title to Jesus Christ who is the theme of the book. Here there are three: faithful witness, the first born from the dead (referring to the resurrection), and the ruler of the earth.

THE PERSONAL DEDICATION OF THE BOOK (1:5b-6)

John dedicates his book "To Him who loved us and washed us from our sins in His own blood, and has made us kings and priests to His God and Father."

Who Loved Us

While not incorrect grammatically to translate "love" in the past tense, it is a present participle in the Greek language: "the one who loves us." His love continues as much for us today as when He loved us on Calvary's cross.

Who Loosed Us

Because of His love the guilt of our sins has been washed away, and we are loosed from the penalty of sin.

Who Lifted Us

Being loved and being free qualifies us for citizenship in God's kingdom as kings and priests.

THE PURPOSE OF THE BOOK (1:7-8)

Verses 7 and 8 are from the inside cover of the "book" we are previewing. In these two verses is found a synopsis of what the book is all about. There are two primary purposes of the Book of Revelation: the presentation of the king and the program of His kingdom.

The Presentation of the King (1:7)

Verse 7 describes in a short sentence the one-day coming again of Jesus Christ. Every eye on earth will see Him and every "tribe" will mourn for Him because of His prior treatment and death in His first coming. The persecuted believers in churches throughout the Roman Empire would have read this verse and taken heart that the Savior who was pierced is coming back to present Himself as king—even king over the Emperor of Rome!

The word "coming" is the Greek word *parousia*. It is the normal word for "coming" or "advent," but came to be applied to the Second Coming of Jesus Christ. This is not the Rapture of the Church; it is Christ's physical appearing in the heavens and on planet earth. More specifically, it refers to a coming which changes the situation into which the coming is made. Like the return of a teacher into a disorderly classroom from which she has been momentarily absent—her coming changes everything. Jesus' *parousia* will make all the difference in the affairs of the world. Whenever God speaks from within a cloud, or uses clouds to accompany His purposes, it is always to make a statement or bring judgment into the situation (Exodus 19:16; 40:34; Daniel 7:13; Matthew 17:5; Acts 1:9). And that is exactly what will happen at Jesus' Second Coming. He will be "coming with clouds" to judge the world. He is not seen by every eye because of television, but because of the radiance of His glory across the heavens. It is hard to imagine what that day will be like.

> *When Jesus was on earth the first time He didn't rule over a small country. He wasn't mayor of a city, governor of a state, or president of Palestine. But someday His kingdom will encompass not only the world, but the entire universe.*
>
> *David Jeremiah*
> ***Escape the Coming Night***

The Program of the Kingdom (1:8)

The program of the kingdom is that Jesus is "the Alpha and the Omega, the Beginning and the End." He is saying, "I am in charge. I just want you to know before I come and while I'm coming and after I've come, I'm the King and I'm in charge." When He uses the words Alpha and Omega, He is using the first and last letter of the Greek alphabet to say, "I am the A-to-Z, the beginning and the end and everything in between."

The beginning and the end has reference not only to the eternality of Christ but also to His authority. He is the One who is totally in charge. His inclusive power, pictured by the expression "Alpha and the Omega" shows He is greater than the process of time. As "the First and the Last," everything we conceive of as "time" is contained in Him. He preceded the creation of the earth and will succeed its re-creation when the new heavens and new earth are set in place. Revelation is the account of Jesus' campaign for the rulership of earth. He was appointed by the Father, won the victory over Satan, and will establish His eternal kingdom when He comes again. He is El Shaddai, "the Almighty."

The message of Revelation is that Jesus is coming back and He is in charge. That's why every believer should study this book until the excitement of Jesus' return begins to grow and bear fruit in him.

APPLICATION

1. Read 2 Peter 3:3–15

   a. What can we anticipate as the time of Christ's appearing draws near? (verses 3–4)

   b. How can the "slow" movement of history be deceiving? (verse 4)

   c. How should we understand the "delay" in Christ's second coming? (verse 9)

   d. What will happen when He returns? (verses 10, 12)

   e. How should we be living in light of His return? (verses 11, 13–14)

   f. What should we be looking forward to? (verse 14)

2. Christ will return to earth as King of Kings. Describe the aspects of His kingship as found in the following verses.

   a. Daniel 4:37

   b. Matthew 2:2

   c. John 1:49

   d. 1 Timothy 1:17

   e. Psalm 24:7

   f. Revelation 15:3

   g. Revelation 19:6

SPEAKING OF THE FUTURE . . .

What would you do if you were the only one in town with a storm cellar, and a tornado was approaching in the distance? No doubt you would act to get your loved ones underground as quickly as possible. You'd get on the telephone, urging every friend and neighbor you could to join you in the storm cellar. Eventually the door would need to be closed. Those inside would escape, but the ones outside would not.

On Sunday, December 26, 2004, a tsunami rolled across the Indian Ocean and killed hundreds of thousands of people in Indonesia and other nations. How do you think the people in those lands would have acted had they received advance warning of the devastation to come? They would have done everything in their power to escape the massive waves.

The prophetic portions of the Bible are like an early warning system for the human race. Judgment is coming upon the earth for all who fail to heed the warning signs that God has been giving for two millennia. The Day of the Lord will come upon us "like a thief in the night" (1 Thessalonians 5:2), but we have been warned ahead of time that the Day is coming.

Are you one who will be found safe in Christ, or one who will fail to heed God's abundant warnings?

FOR THIS CAUSE EVERYONE WHO IS GODLY SHALL PRAY TO YOU IN A TIME
WHEN YOU MAY BE FOUND; SURELY IN A FLOOD OF GREAT WATERS
THEY SHALL NOT COME NEAR HIM.

—David in Psalm 32:6

CHRIST AND HIS CHURCHES

Revelation 1:9-20

In this lesson we meet the risen, glorified, soon-to-come King of Kings.

You will find more in-depth information on this lesson in the book *Escape the Coming Night*, chapter 3.

OUTLINE

Many images of Jesus exist in our world. Artists and authors have contributed to the collection, and each person has his own concept of who He is. The next picture the world sees of Jesus Christ will be one they've never seen before—one that caused John to fall down as dead.

I. **This Vision Was Seen by John While in Exile**

II. **This Vision Was Received by John While in the Spirit**

III. **This Vision Was to Be Written by John and Sent to the Seven Churches**

IV. **This Vision Is of the Glorified, Risen Son of Man**
   A. The Position of Christ in the Vision
   B. The Portrait of Christ in the Vision

V. **This Vision Paralyzed John Until Touched by the Lord**
   A. Fear Not, for I Am the Eternal God
   B. Fear Not, for I Am the Resurrected Christ
   C. Fear Not, for I Have the Keys of Death and Hell

Artists through the centuries have offered many variations on the theme of the physical appearance of Jesus of Nazareth. Unfortunately, too often they have made Him appear as a European or Scandinavian Jesus instead of a Jewish Jesus. While the four Gospels offer no clues as to what Jesus looked like, we assume that He probably looked like an average Jewish man of His day.

But even if we were to create an accurate representation of what He looked like when He walked the earth as a man, that appearance is nothing like what the Apostle John saw on the island of Patmos. Jesus Christ appeared to John in His glorified state as King and Lord of all, not the lowly Galilean of His first coming. He stood before John as the Judge, the Lion of Judah, not the gentle Lamb of God. With eyes like flames of fire and a voice like the sound of many waters, the Jesus of Revelation is an awesome figure. And well we should study His appearance since that is the Jesus we will one day see and worship.

THIS VISION WAS SEEN BY JOHN WHILE IN EXILE (1:9)

John penned Revelation while in the same condition under which many of the Bible's authors wrote: suffering. Think of Moses in the wilderness, David fleeing from Saul, Isaiah persecuted by kings, Ezekiel in exile, Jeremiah being persecuted, and Paul in all sorts of tribulation and trials. Suffering is the common lot of God's people in this age, as exemplified by the experience of the suffering Servant/Savior Himself. As John wrote he was in exile on the island of Patmos in the Aegean Sea, being punished by the Roman Emperor Domitian for his Christian testimony. The historian Tacitus says "the sea was thickly strewn with exiles in those days. The crags were stained with the blood of victims."

Verse 9 says it was "for [on account of] the word of God and for the testimony of Jesus Christ" that John was exiled. Sir William Ramsay, noted historian of the New Testament period, says exile was "preceded by scourging, marked by perpetual fetters, scanty clothing, insufficient food, sleep on the bare ground in a dark prison, and work under the lash of military overseers."[1] Yet in the midst of that dark setting the Word of God came to John, and the glory of the risen Lord was shown to him. John was the last of the living apostles and the leader of the believers in Asia Minor, living in Ephesus. There is no small irony in the fact that the disciple "whom Jesus loved" (John 13:23; 20:2; 21:7, 20) did not escape tribulation for the sake of his Beloved.

THIS VISION WAS RECEIVED BY JOHN WHILE IN THE SPIRIT (1:10)

The phrase "in *the* Spirit" is used often in Christian circles today, often without much accompanying definition. John uses the phrase several times in Revelation (1:10; 4:2; 17:3; 21:10) and it is usually plain what he means. While we say "in the Spirit," John's words actually are that he "became in Spirit"—in other words, he was "Spirit-ized." I think what he means is that instead of functioning within the normal constraints of time and space, he functioned in the additional dimension of the spirit realm. He moved upward to see things in Heaven and move forward to see things in time.

Aleksandr Solzhenitsyn, who knew both the terror of imprisonment and the humiliation of exile, wrote: "Arrest! Need it be said that it is a breaking point in your life, a bolt of lightning which has scored a direct hit on you? It is an unassimilable spiritual earthquake not every person can cope with, as a result of which people often slip into insanity." John [did not go] insane; he was the one person God entrusted to reveal the end of this present age and the beginning of a new world.

David Jeremiah
Escape the Coming Night

He says he was "in Spirit" on "the Lord's Day," a term we use to refer to Sunday, when the church meets together. While that may be what John meant, there are some complications with that view. First, we might wonder how John managed to receive and write down the entire Book of Revelation in one Lord's Day. Second, "Sunday" was never called by the name "the Lord's Day" elsewhere in the New Testament; it is always called "the first day of the week" meaning the day Christ was resurrected (Matthew 28:1; Luke 24:1; John 20:1, 19; Acts 20:7; 1 Corinthians 16:2). The alternative is to view John referring not to "the Lord's Day" but to "the Day of the Lord." That seems more likely—that John is relating something beyond the bounds of a 24-hour day. Rather, he is referring to the broad scope of the Day of the Lord, all those things that transpire when God brings human history to a climax culminating with the Second Coming of Christ. Being "in Spirit" is the only way to see such an expanse of human history, so the two references to being in Spirit in the Day of the Lord complement each other nicely.

This Vision Was to Be Written by John and Sent to the Seven Churches (1:11-12)

Every time John receives a vision he is told to write it down—12 times, to be exact. He is also told specifically whom to send the contents of his visions to: "the seven churches which are in Asia." The churches are represented by seven golden lampstands.

Lampstands are a symbol of light and are used to illuminate the darkness. They are useless during the day, but when the night comes they are essential. Jesus said the night was coming when no man can work (John 9:4). His being rejected by the world was the beginning of that darkness which will be removed upon His return. But in the absence of His presence, His Church is to be the light of the world, declaring His presence in the midst of darkness. So it is to the church, represented corporately by seven churches in Asia Minor, to whom John will send the record of the revelation.

This Vision Is of the Glorified, Risen Son of Man (1:13-16)

In the midst of the circle of golden lampstands John sees Jesus Christ—and follows with a detailed description of the glorified, risen Lord. While others in the Bible encountered the Lord in different circumstances, none were commanded to write down what they saw so as to be read by others. What John saw is for all of us—he was commanded to write down and send it to the churches. The term "Son of Man" speaks of the Son of God as the God-Man, deity in human form. Jesus used that term scores of times to describe Himself in the Gospels.

The Position of Christ in the Vision

We have a wonderful picture of Christ in the midst of His body, the church, represented by the golden lampstands. It is a picture of what He said in Matthew 18:20, "For where two or three are gathered together in my name, there am I in the midst of them." Jesus wants to be in the center of the life of His church.

The Portrait of Christ in the Vision

The picture of Christ arising out of John's vision is given to us in human terms, but it is also symbolic of who He is.

1. His clothing

    Two parts of His clothing are mentioned. First, a long flowing robe speaks of His greatness (compare the robe Isaiah saw in Isaiah 6:1, a robe that filled the temple). Second, He had a golden girdle wrapped around His breast which speaks of His righteousness (Isaiah 11:5). He no longer girds Himself with a towel as a servant (John 13:4-5), but now with the righteousness of a King.

2. His head and hair

The whiteness of His hair speaks of His eternity or His duration. It is not the whiteness of old age but of absolute holiness. Like the white wigs worn by British judges, whiteness symbolizes the purity of judgment (Daniel 7:9-13).

3. His eyes

John probably remembered Jesus' eyes being filled with compassion, even tears, when on earth. But now His eyes are like flames of fire, penetrating to the deepest part of the soul. There is nothing hidden from the gaze of His eyes (Psalm 11:4; Hebrews 4:13). Those who believe they can hide anything from God will have it all revealed by the vision of the Son of Man.

4. His feet

Brass in the Bible always speaks of judgment, and feet of brass symbolizes the time when Christ will put all his enemies under His feet in judgment. The feet of the One who brought the Gospel (Isaiah 52:7; Romans 10:15) are now the feet of the Judge of those who rejected the Gospel.

5. His mouth

Two aspects are important here: the sound of His voice and the content of His voice. His voice sounds like the roar of many waters and signifies the power and far-reaching impact of His voice (Psalm 29:4; Ezekiel 43:2). His voice of judgment will be heard throughout the earth. But it is what He will say that is so important. John sees a sharp, two-edged sword coming out of His mouth. The sword is obviously the Word of God (Ephesians 6:17; Hebrews 4:12) and represents God's ultimate weapon. That sword is what He will ultimately use to judge the nations (Revelation 19:15, 21).

6. His hands

The right hand always speaks of lordship, control, and authority. The seven stars He holds in His right hand are the messengers of the seven churches (1:20). "Messengers" comes from the same Greek word as does "angels," and in reality the stars represent angels sent to preach to the seven churches. Those who are sent, even today, as preachers of the Word to the churches of Jesus Christ are held in the place of authority by the Lord Jesus Christ—in His right hand (Daniel 12:3).

7. His face

John saw the face of Jesus on the Mount of Transfiguration (Matthew 17:2), and His face now appears as it did that day, shining like the sun. This has to be the bright light, brighter than the sun, Paul saw when he was converted (Acts 26:13). We will see in our study of Revelation that by the time Christ appears at His Second Coming all other sources of light will be gone—the sun, moon, and stars. His face alone will illuminate a dark and sinful world, brighter even than the brightness of the sun.

> *Friend, this is the Jesus . . . who not only knows the future, but who lives in it just as comfortably as He lives in what has been. This is the Jesus who holds all power in His hands, and yet who bids us draw near and walk with Him. And this is the Jesus who sees everything that lies ahead for every one of us and who says to us all, "Do not be afraid!"*
>
> *David Jeremiah,*
> ***Jesus' Final Warning***

The composite picture of Jesus Christ in all the varied components is of a Lord who is coming as the Holy One to purge His Church (2:16, 18, 23). We are relieved that we do not have to stand before such a one as this at the Great White Throne judgment. But we forget that we do have to appear before Him at the judgment seat of Christ to have our work for Him evaluated. We should not be surprised if our reaction in that day is the same as John had on the island of Patmos.

THIS VISION PARALYZED JOHN UNTIL TOUCHED BY THE LORD

John fell at the feet of Jesus "as dead." It is overwhelming enough to read about His appearance without seeing it in person. Perhaps some of John's shock was the way Jesus' appearance had changed since the last time he saw Him. John had seen the resurrected Christ but not the glorified King of Kings. His awesome majesty notwithstanding, Jesus reaches out to comfort the disciple whom He had loved, and loved still. Jesus reached out with the right hand of His power and touched John to comfort him. He told John not to fear for three reasons.

Fear Not, for I Am the Eternal God

Because Jesus is "the First and the Last," that is the same as being "the Only." There is no other with greater power or authority. Jesus is the eternal God.

Fear Not, for I Am the Resurrected Christ

Because Jesus is alive from the dead, and alive for evermore, He serves to make intercession forever for us (Hebrews 7:25). He is our eternal, living advocate before the Father and holds our future in His hands.

Fear Not, for I Have the Keys of Death and Hell

Human destiny is in His hands. Christ alone controls the doors of death and hell, and we have no reason to fear that terrible destiny if we are in Him.

The awesome Christ whom John met on the island of Patmos is the Christ about to be revealed to the world. May we be in preparation for the day we will see Him, as John did, face to face.

APPLICATION

1. What did the Apostle Paul say regarding the hardships that Christians can expect to suffer? (Acts 14:22b)

   a. What was a large part of his ministry devoted to? (Acts 14:22a)

   b. What words of advice (warning) did he give to his protégé Timothy? (2 Timothy 3:12)

   c. Who besides apostles should expect to suffer for Christ? (2 Timothy 3:12)

   d. Jesus appeared to John to reveal the future to him at a time when John was suffering. What sense of "normalcy" does that give to suffering?

   e. Do you see any indication that Jesus is about to release John from exile on Patmos?

   f. Rather than feeling "set aside" during times of suffering for our faith, what does John's experience teach us?

2. Record your insights about Christ's appearance as gleaned from the following verses of Scripture.

   a. His clothing (Isaiah 6:1; John 13:4-5)

   b. His hair (Daniel 7:9-13)

   c. His eyes (Psalm 11:4; Hebrews 4:13)

d. His feet (Isaiah 52:7; Romans 10:15)

e. His mouth (Psalm 29:4; 93:4; Jeremiah 25:30-31; Ezekiel 43:2; Ephesians 6:17; Hebrews 4:12; Revelation 2:16; 19:15, 21)

f. His hands (Daniel 12:3; Ephesians 1:20)

g. His face (Matthew 17:2; Acts 9:1-5; 2 Peter 1:19; Revelation 22:16)

SPEAKING OF THE FUTURE . . .

Henry Venn, an eighteenth century Anglican clergyman in England, was from a long line of distinguished churchmen. He served several parishes and was esteemed as a preacher and writer. It is said that when he was on his deathbed, the prospect of meeting the Savior put him in such high spirits that it actually boosted his health. His biographer wrote, "His joy at dying kept him alive a further fortnight."

How is it that anyone could take joy at the prospect of dying? It is possible only for those who know the prophetic promises of the Bible. Prophecy looks to the future and promises complete transformation and victory. Those who live in the best of circumstances in this life know that it is "far better" to ultimately live with Christ. The day is coming when He will rule over all the earth, and the saints of God will share in His glory and presence. Satan, the enemy of God, will be brought to heel and ultimately imprisoned forever. Who wouldn't be excited about death if they knew it was the doorway to victory with Jesus?

One way to have a full life on this earth is to be filled with joy at the anticipation of meeting Jesus.

> FOR I AM HARD PRESSED BETWEEN THE TWO, HAVING A DESIRE
> TO DEPART AND BE WITH CHRIST, WHICH IS FAR BETTER.
> —Paul in Philippians 1:23

Note:

[1] William Ramsay, *The Letters to the Seven Churches* (Grand Rapids: Baker Book House, 1963), 85.

LOSING OUR FIRST LOVE: EPHESUS

Revelation 2:1-7

In this lesson we discover why a church is only as strong as its love for Christ.

You will find more in-depth information on this lesson in the book *Escape the Coming Night*, chapter 4, pages 53-58.

OUTLINE

It's easy to look at a church from the outside and think it has few faults. It can be energetic, committed, goal-oriented, on track, and careful about the letter of the law. But what kind of heart beats inside that well-oiled machine? Jesus always looks beneath the surface.

   I. **The Destination of the Letter**

  II. **The Description of Christ**

 III. **The Diagnosis of the Church**
        A. It Was a Dynamic Church
        B. It Was a Dedicated Church
        C. It Was a Determined Church
        D. It Was a Disciplined Church
        E. It Was a Discerning Church

 IV. **The Demands Made to the Church**
        A. Remember
        B. Repent
        C. Repeat

C hapter two of the Book of Revelation begins the second of the three sections of the book as outlined in 1:19. Chapter one, as you recall from Lesson 2 in this series, constituted "the things which you have seen." Chapter one of Revelation records the things John says when confronted by the Lord Jesus Christ. Beginning in chapter four, we have the future vision which is "the things which will take place after this."

In between chapters one and four are "the things which are"— comprising chapters two and three. These "things" are the messages to the seven churches of Asia, but which are applicable to the church in the present age as well. Though the Book of Revelation was to go to all seven churches, these shorter, individual letters were addressed by Christ to the separate churches. Seven brief messages for seven churches—and to the church of today.

Before looking at the first letter to the church in Ephesus, let's note three different perspectives on these letters we must keep in mind as we are reading them:

1. They must be understood in their primary association. These are real letters written to seven literal churches of Asia Minor at the end of the first century A.D. (the churches are listed in Revelation 1:11). As well as expected differences, there are similarities in the letters. Each begins with "I know your works" and each has a promise "to him who overcomes." But each one's message is tailored to the needs of the church to which it is addressed. Each letter must be read in its own context.

2. They must be understood in their personal application. The great value of these letters beyond the first century is in identifying the kinds of Christians who show up in the church in every age. As we study the contents of these letters you will likely think of individuals or churches which manifest the characteristics described. These letters are tests for the modern church. The Lord with the eyes of fire is searching the heart of His churches to see who they really are. To get the perspective of the Head of the church on the church itself will be revealing—and convicting. Problems faced by modern churches could be solved by reading the recommendations of the Lord to the seven churches in Asia. It's interesting that all seven churches got to read the short letters written to each of the other churches since they were all contained in the Book of Revelation they received from John. We have the same advantage today.

3. They must be understood in their prophetic anticipation. Many conservative Bible students believe the seven churches, in the order they are addressed by Christ, have come to be a prophetic picture of the chronological development of the universal Church spiritually. Thus, the first church, Ephesus, would be a picture of the church in apostolic days and the last church, Laodicea, would represent the church just before the return of Christ. We look at this chronological, spiritual progression after concluding our study of the letters to all seven churches.

We turn our attention now to the first of the seven letters, addressed to the church at Ephesus (2:1-7): the church without love.

THE DESTINATION OF THE LETTER

The letter is addressed to the angel, or messenger, of the church at Ephesus—probably a reference to the pastor. Ephesus was the most prominent city in Roman Asia Minor, a religious and commercial center for that part of the world. It was cosmopolitan and cultured, filled with the rich and poor alike. It was home to one of the seven wonders of the world, the Temple of Diana, able to seat 24,000 people at one time. The temple was a center of immorality, a bank, and an art gallery. Great revenue was derived from the sale of statues of Diana.

Paul established a church in Ephesus on his second missionary journey, and later spent three years there. The letter which we know as Ephesians was written by Paul to the Christian church in that city. Paul had established Timothy as the pastor of the church, and the two letters Paul wrote to Timothy were received by him while he was pastor in Ephesus. It is likely that John the apostle became the head of the church there following Timothy's ministry. It was while John was living in Ephesus that he was taken captive and exiled to Patmos.

THE DESCRIPTION OF CHRIST

It is fascinating to discover that as Christ delivers His message to each of the seven churches, He focuses on one aspect of His own character as revealed in Revelation, chapter one (discussed in our last lesson), and applies that aspect of His character to the church He is addressing. For instance, in the second letter, to the church at Smyrna, He introduces Himself as "the First and the Last, who was dead, and came to life" (Revelation 2:8). That description of Christ is taken directly from the description of Himself in 1:17-18. It is that aspect of Christ's identity which will meet the need of the church in Smyrna. It is like that with all seven of the churches. The point is that the person and character of Christ is sufficient to meet every need the church may have.

To the church at Ephesus Christ is portrayed as the One "who holds the seven stars in His right hand, who walks in the midst of the seven golden lampstands" (2:1). He is saying to the church that no matter what their problems, in His authoritative right hand is the power to meet their needs.

THE DIAGNOSIS OF THE CHURCH (2:2-3)

In every church there is good news and bad news. The good news about Ephesus takes up most of Christ's words to them. There were five positive things mentioned about the church at Ephesus, with one negative characteristic mentioned at the end.

The Ephesian congregation was dynamic and its annual report must have looked good. It would never have matched this report I saw recently: "Annual report... New Members: None. Baptisms: None. Gifts to Missions: None." Then, at the bottom of the report, the church clerk had written, "Brethren, pray for us that we might be faithful unto the end."

David Jeremiah
Escape the Coming Night

It Was a Dynamic Church

The Ephesus church was a busy, working, dynamic congregation, doing the work of the Lord. We often de-emphasize the importance of works because we don't want to water down the importance of grace in our salvation. But wherever you find a clear message of grace being preached you also find a working church. People who understand grace biblically also abound in works for the Lord (Ephesians 2:8-10). The Word of God was spreading throughout Asia as a result of the activities for the Gospel in Ephesus (Acts 19:10). Many churches spend their whole existence in a maintenance mode instead of a mission mode. They just maintain something that somebody else started. But that was not true in Ephesus. The church of Jesus Christ was dynamic in that place and they are commended for it.

It Was a Dedicated Church

There is a difference between "works" and "labor" in verse 2. Labor means work to the point of exhaustion. That is, the Ephesians were paying a price to serve the Lord. There is even a hint of weariness in this word; the Ephesians were exhausted from their labor. I see this often in our church, lay people who spend 40-60 hours a week at their own jobs and tending to the needs of their families and then still investing additional hours in the work of the ministry. Unfortunately, there are always too few in the body of Christ at large willing to pay that kind of price. But there were people like that in Ephesus.

King David of Israel is an example of service that costs something. He said, "Nor will I offer burnt offerings to the LORD my God with that which costs me nothing" (2 Samuel 24:24). With paid staff present in most churches today, it is easy for members to think that everything will get done without them. Apparently that perspective was not true in Ephesus—the church labored at a cost.

It Was a Determined Church

The word "patience" occurs twice with reference to the church at Ephesus, once in verse 2 concerning their service and again in verse 3 regarding their suffering. They were a church that did not give up. This is the kind of patience that endures but maintains its forward motion. This wasn't suffering under a pile waiting for persecution or service to pass. This was patience as they served and as they suffered for the sake of the Gospel. In Acts 19 we read of the fierce opposition the church at Ephesus encountered. They were hated and despised, but they did not give up. They were patient in their afflictions. Christians like the Ephesians get better the tougher things get.

It Was a Disciplined Church

The church at Ephesus was a church which could not bear "those who are evil" (2:2). They would not tolerate evil in their midst and practiced church discipline whenever necessary. They were patient when it came to service and suffering, but not when it came to sinning! Church discipline is a lost practice in most Christian churches today. There is such a threat of lawsuits if churches do anything to a member which even hints of discipline that many pastors are afraid to raise issues of sin. But to be a church that is obedient to the

> *Pray God to send a few men with what the Americans call 'grit' in them; men, who, when they know a thing to be right, will not turn away, or turn aside, or stop; men, who will persevere all the more because there are difficulties to meet or foes to encounter; who stand all the more true to their Master because they are opposed; who, the more they are thrust into the fire, the hotter they become; who just like the bow, the further the string is drawn, the more powerfully it sends forth its arrows, and so the more they are trodden upon, the more mighty will they become in the cause of truth against error.*
>
> *Charles H. Spurgeon*

Word of God, church discipline must be carried out. It is better to obey God than men (Acts 5:29). God will not bless churches which tolerate sin in their midst.

It Was a Discerning Church

To the Ephesians' credit, they were a church which fought hard to remain pure in doctrine. They would not allow into their church those who claimed to have apostolic authority but were not true apostles. Historians tell us that, up until about A.D. 150 there were some church leaders who traveled about claiming to have been appointed by one of the 12 original apostles—a practice gradually called Apostolic Succession. They would claim to have inherited the authority and power—and therefore the "rights"—of the apostle who "ordained" them. But the Ephesians would have none of it. They barred these false apostles from the church. In addition to keeping out these false apostles, the Ephesian church neither gave room to a group called the Nicolaitans (2:6). There is no certainty as to the identity of this group, but some feel they advocated a distinction between the "clergy" and the "laity" in the early church, diminishing the doctrine of the priesthood of all believers. Others believe they were the followers of one Nicolaus from Antioch, a man who promoted immoral and impure lifestyles for believers. In any case, the Ephesians would not tolerate the Nicolaitans' influence in their church.

Externally, the Ephesians were a commendable church in every way. But the gaze of King Jesus went beneath the surface and found an area in which they were lacking: They had left their first love (2:4). Leaving one's first love means losing the excitement and devotion a new believer experiences when first born again. It's getting over the honeymoon and allowing Christianity to become a religion instead of a relationship. The Ephesians had this one fault. And, because they did not love Jesus, they likely weren't loving each other.

THE DEMANDS MADE TO THE CHURCH

Jesus' diagnosis is followed by His three-part prescription: Remember, repent, repeat (2:5).

Remember

Restoration begins by remembering—meditating on what your relationship with Christ was like when you first were saved. Remembering how you used to witness for Him. Remembering what it was like to lead someone to the Lord. Remembering what it was like to trust Him with the simplest, and the greatest, of your needs.

Repent

Repentance means changing your mind and turning to go in the opposite direction. If you have left your first love you must turn and head back to Him. That requires a choice and an act of the will on your part.

Repeat

"Do the first works" means to begin doing again the faithful steps of discipleship that you took as a new believer. Feelings follow actions, not vice versa. Where the body goes, the heart will follow. Trust that your obedience to do the "first works" will be followed by a heart that gets emotionally excited once again.

The thought of any church's light being removed because it left its first love is a frightening thought, so much so that every church member should look within and see if he or she has left his or her first love.

APPLICATION

1. Read the account of Paul in Ephesus in Acts 19.

    a. Where did Paul usually go first on his journeys? (verse 8)

    b. What was the result of Paul's extended stay in Ephesus? (verse 10)

    c. What happened through Paul which probably had an impact on the acceptance of the Gospel? (verse 11)

    d. What experience did the disciples gain with false "believers?" (verses 13-16)

    e. What was the result of the "power encounters" associated with Paul's visit? (verses 18-20)

    f. What economic impact did the Gospel have on Ephesus? (verses 23-27)

    g. What persecution did some of Paul's friends experience at the hands of the citizens of Ephesus? (verses 28-41)

    h. How does this background aid in understanding the commendation Christ gave to the church of Ephesus in Revelation 2:1-7?

2. In spite of being saved by grace through faith, what are Christians saved for? (Ephesians 2:8-10)

    a. What kinds of works did the average church in the first-century Roman Empire have to engage in to remain faithful to Christ?

3. What advice did Paul give the believers in Corinth, another
location where ridicule of Christianity was great?
(1 Corinthians 15:58)

a. How much experience does the average Christian church in
America have with being "steadfast . . . immovable?"

4. How does one learn to discern good from evil? (Hebrews 5:14)

a. How many times has your church exercised church discipline
against someone who was sinning as a Christian?

b. How does it weaken the church in the long run if discipline is
not carried out?

SPEAKING OF THE FUTURE . . .

Followers of Jesus have speculated about the time of His return to earth since He first made it plain that He wasn't going away forever. In fact, the original disciples thought Jesus' resurrection might be His second coming: "Lord, will You at this time restore the kingdom to Israel?" (Acts 1:6) It is obvious from their perplexed looks that when He did ascend out of sight, they were confused. It took two angels to give them reassurance that Jesus would return— but they didn't tell the disciples the time.

Many modern Bible students have tried to set the date of Christ's second coming and failed. If they had read Mark 13:32, they would not have set themselves up for such a fall: "But of that day and hour no one knows, not even the angels in heaven, nor the Son, but only the Father." Instead of guessing the day of Jesus' return, believers should be consumed with two tasks: watching for signs of the times (Luke 21:11, 25; 1 Thessalonians 5:6) and working diligently as faithful stewards (1 Corinthians 15:58). Our motivation while we wait is knowing our works will be examined by Christ and our faithfulness rewarded (1 Corinthians 3:11–15; 2 Corinthians 5:10).

Every Christian should be bivocational: watching for the Lord in whose service we work until His appearing.

WATCH, STAND FAST IN THE FAITH, BE BRAVE, BE STRONG.
—Paul in 1 Corinthians 16:13

THE SUFFERING CHURCH: SMYRNA

Revelation 2:8-11

In this lesson we discover how to have everything when we have nothing.

You will find more in-depth information on this lesson in the book *Escape the Coming Night*, chapter 4, pages 58-61.

OUTLINE

American believers rarely experience economic deprivation because of their faith. What would happen if we suddenly lost "everything" on account of our testimony for Christ? We would need to read the letter to the church at Smyrna, for whom such testing was a way of life.

   I. **The Church**

  II. **Why the Church in Smyrna Suffered**
     A. Pressure
     B. Poverty
     C. Persecution

 III. **The Lord's Counsel to the Church**
     A. Be Fearless and Faithful
     B. One Fearless and Faithful Man

The second church to receive a letter from Christ through John the apostle was the church of Smyrna. Founded around 1000 B.C., it had been destroyed in 600 B.C. and rebuilt centuries later by one of Alexander the Great's generals. It was a matter of pride to the city that it had died and risen to live again.

Smyrna was considered the most beautiful city the Greeks ever built. It sat on a hill rising from the sea so that it looked as if the city wore a crown. Smyrna was called "The Glory of Asia" because of its pride and beauty. During the Roman period, Caesar-worship in Asia was centered there. The city was a place of wisdom, beauty, and commerce—and also the location of the church of Jesus Christ.

THE CHURCH

We know little of the founding of the church in Smyrna, but we do know they suffered great persecution for the sake of Christ. The letter of Christ to Smyrna is the shortest of the seven letters, and contains no condemnation at all. All that is said to the church in Smyrna is positive and encouraging. We will understand Christ's words to the church better if we understand exactly why they were suffering.

WHY THE CHURCH IN SMYRNA SUFFERED

The church was no doubt despised by the city because of its insignificance. A street in Smyrna called "the street of the gods" was lined with temples to Greek and Roman deities—beautifully ornate structures which competed with each other for glory and acclaim. Compared to these ornate facades, the Christians met in the plainest of places—homes, tombs, outdoors, wherever they could find a quiet place to gather. They had nothing to boast of when it came to temples.

Another reason for their suffering is found in understanding emperor-worship in the Roman period. Today we consider the Roman Empire a brutal and tyrannical government, but the citizens of the day didn't feel that way at all. The Pax Romana, the peace of Rome, which extended throughout the Mediterranean World, removed the threat of wars. And for that the citizens were grateful. Rome's strength guaranteed peace and safety. There were laws, there were roads, there was commerce; most Roman citizens were happy with their lot in life. Emperor-worship grew out of a patriotic and grateful attitude on the part of the people for what

Rome provided them. It was political, not religious, worship. While emperors resisted the idea at first, by the time Revelation was written, emperor-worship was compulsory throughout the empire. In fact, John's banishment to Patmos was a result of his unwillingness to worship the emperor Domitian. To fail to worship the emperor was to be an ungrateful and unpatriotic member of the Roman Empire. Therefore Christians were in constant jeopardy for being "bad citizens." They were tortured on the rack, boiled in oil, roasted over slow fires, crucified, and fed to ravenous beasts—all as a form of entertainment for the true citizens of Rome.

Christ says to the church in Smyrna that He knows of their "works, tribulation, and poverty . . . and . . . the blasphemy of those who say they are Jews and are not, but are a synagogue of Satan"—all experienced while being faithful to Christ under Roman oppression.

> *Corrie ten Boom, the Dutch woman who saved Jews from the Gestapo, recalled a childhood incident when she told her father, "I am afraid that I will never be strong enough to die as a martyr." He said, "When you have to go on a journey, when do I give you the money for the fare—two weeks before?" "No Daddy, on the day that I am leaving." "Precisely . . . and our wise Father in heaven knows when we're going to need things, too. When the time comes to die, you will find the strength you need—just in time."*
>
> David Jeremiah
> **Escape the Coming Night**

Pressure

The word for tribulation is the Greek word *thlipsis*, which means "pressure." It is an unrelenting pressure, like having a boulder on your chest which causes you to suffocate slowly. The pressure the Christians were under was like that—slow, unrelenting, never-ending, day after day pressure from the Roman Empire to conform to their ways. We do not know today what it is like to live under that kind of pressure where physical torture might be the end result at any moment.

Poverty

Two words designated poverty in the New Testament: *penes* (compare the English "penny") meant poor in the sense of working daily for daily wages to earn a living. The second word is *ptocheia* which meant abject poverty or destitution—someone with no resources whatever. This was the word Jesus used to describe the poverty of the Christians in Smyrna. In the midst of Smyrna, "the Glory of Asia," they had absolutely nothing. Their poverty was due to their faith. They would have been robbed and looted, treated like outcasts, and kept from getting any kind of meaningful employment, all because of their lack of loyalty to the emperor.

Persecution

The word "blasphemy" might be better rendered "slander." There was a group of unbelieving Jews in Smyrna who had perhaps been converted to the traditions of Judaism but were interested in the "grace" of Christianity as well. This syncretistic mixture of beliefs found fertile ground in the religious soil of Asia Minor. The Romans were tolerant of religious belief as long as priority worship was given to the emperor. So in the post-apostolic age all kinds of Jewish-Christian syncretism grew up in the area where the seven churches were located. And here Christ says the believers were being slandered by a group of "non-Jewish" Jews, "a synagogue of Satan."

The church at Smyrna was under a daily load of pressure, poverty, and persecution from a false cult. They needed counsel from the Lord on how to survive, counsel which can prove valuable to us as well.

THE LORD'S COUNSEL TO THE CHURCH

In verse 10, the Lord gives two overall commands to the believers in Smyrna: be fearless and be faithful. This was not a trite rubber-stamp solution to their needs. We will discover the underlying reasons why fearlessness and faithfulness will see us through pressure, poverty, and persecution.

Be Fearless and Faithful

If you were pressured, poor, and persecuted in Smyrna, what good would it do to be told just to be fearless and faithful. Is that really a solution? It is if we look carefully at what Jesus said. He said don't fear "any of those things which you are about to suffer." Not just "don't be afraid" in general, but "don't be afraid of the specific things you are facing." This is like David saying that he would walk through the valley of the shadow of death but he would not fear. So the Christians in Smyrna were not to fear what pressure, poverty, or persecution could do to them.

Jesus also says in verse 10 to "be faithful unto death." When the pressure comes, we want to run. But Jesus says our calling is to remain right in the middle of the pressure, poverty, and persecution and be faithful. It would be easier for all of us to find places to live and work where there wasn't so much pressure. But Christ says we are to stay put and stay faithful. Why? Why should we be fearless and faithful until the end? There are five reasons which can be deduced from what Jesus says to the church at Smyrna:

1. The reputation of Christ was better than the reputation of Rome.

   Jesus addressed the church as "the First and the Last, who was dead, and came to life," a reference back to the description of Him in 1:17-18. The church at Smyrna needed to know that the One who transcends all time and space, and who is more powerful than death itself, was the One who was over their lives. Because Christ is the beginning and the end, He is there in the midst of the persecution in Smyrna. The power of the citizens of Smyrna would have come to the believers' minds with Christ's words. Their city was the first and last word of culture and beauty in Asia. They had risen from the dust of their own ashes. And yet Christ is greater than all the Greek and Roman nobility they could muster. The Romans had a first and last and resurrected city, but the believers knew the One who was the true First and Last, the One who was raised from the dead. The reputation of their Lord was far better than the reputation of Rome.

2. The recognition of Christ was better than the recognition of Rome.

   A tiny Greek word, *oida*, held huge meaning for the believers in Smyrna: "I know. . . ." Christ knows what they are going through. If you ever wonder if anyone knows what you are going through, there is Someone who does, and His name is Jesus. Whether any other person knows or not doesn't matter, as long as Jesus knows. *Oida* doesn't mean to know intellectually only. It means to know by virtue of experience. Jesus is saying to them that He has been where they are: pressured, poor, and

> *He took cognizance of every sorrow; His heart felt every pang; he counted every tear. The weight of oppression was fully known to Him, and the wealth of His divine sympathy went out to His people . . . and still today, not a trial passes unnoticed, nor a difficulty unobserved. Our great shepherd knows every bruise sustained by His sheep, and every suffering experienced by them, and because He too has passed through suffering, He sympathizes with his own.*
>
> *Fred Tatford*

persecuted. The believers in Smyrna were not recognized by anybody in the city, but they were recognized by Christ.

3. The riches of Christ were better than the riches of Rome.

Why does Jesus say the believers at Smyrna were poverty-stricken and rich at the same time? It's because He is speaking out of a totally different value system. The economics of the kingdom of heaven are the opposite of the kingdoms of this world—like someone switched all the price tags in a hardware store over night. The church in Laodicea was a church that had the world's value system. They were rich in worldly goods but Christ says they are "wretched, miserable, poor, blind, and naked" (3:17). Smyrna was poor but rich; Laodicea was rich but poor. We will learn in a future lesson that the church in Laodicea represents the end-time church, rich in things of the material world. But the Smyrna church was the persecuted church to whom Christ gave special attention because of their poverty in this world.

4. The reckoning of time by Christ was better than the reckoning of time by Rome.

In a further word, Jesus warns the believers in Smyrna that they haven't seen anything yet—they are about to be thrown into prison for "ten days." What is the meaning of this? Some think the "ten days" represents 10 years of suffering to come, but most think otherwise. First, remember that God doesn't keep time like we do (a day is as a thousand years; 2 Peter 3:8), and I don't think He was referring to a specific amount of time. I think he used "ten days" to represent a short time from the perspective of the believers in Smyrna. Not ten literal days, but a day that, from the perspective of heaven, was a short time—a time they could endure with His help. No suffering is too much to endure when the Lord is with us. His "time" takes precedence over ours.

5. The rewards of Christ are better than the rewards of Rome.

Finally, the rewards of heaven are far better than the rewards of this earth. The crown of eternal life was promised by Jesus to

> "I thank you that you have graciously thought me worthy of this day and of this hour, that I may be a part of the number of martyrs to die for Christ."
> Polycarp, pastor of the church at Smyrna, on the day of his martyrdom.
>
> David Jeremiah
> *Escape the Coming Night*

the believers at Smyrna for those who remained "faithful until death." Receiving the crown of life is a shield against the threat of the "second death," eternal separation from God. What can the world offer that matches that?

ONE FEARLESS AND FAITHFUL MAN

The pastor of the church in Smyrna was Polycarp, a disciple, history tells us, of the Apostle John himself. In February of A.D. 156 Polycarp was one of 11 Christians who was tortured and then thrown to the beasts by the Romans. Both Jews and Romans participated in his killing. He was burned at the stake. Given the opportunity to deny Christ, instead he welcomed the flames that consumed him, counting it an honor to die for the One who died for him.

The only way Polycarp could have died such a death was by believing the things written to his church by Jesus in the Book of Revelation. And that is the only way we can live for Him as well.

APPLICATION

1. Read Hebrews 4:14-16.

   a. What is Jesus to us? (verse 14)

   b. What should we do in light of who He is? (verse 14)

   c. What does the exhortation to "hold fast" imply about the temptation to do otherwise?

   d. Why is Jesus able to say "I know" concerning what we are going through? (verse 15)

   e. What difference does that make in our prayer life during times of pressure, poverty, or persecution? (verse 16)

2. How did Paul explain his own state of riches or poverty? (2 Corinthians 6:10)

   a. Which did he prefer? (Philippians 4:11-12)

   b. What were his true riches? (Philippians 4:13, 19)

   c. What did Christ do to demonstrate the truth about riches? (2 Corinthians 8:9)

   d. Why did He become poor?

3. Read 2 Corinthians 4:16-18.

   a. Why should we not lose heart in times of trouble? (verse 16)

   b. What is the "weight" of our affliction in God's terms? (verse 17a)

   c. How long does it last from God's perspective? (verse 17a)

   d. How "heavy" is the glory which our light affliction leads to?
   (verse 17b)

   e. How should we learn to "see" while living in this world?
   (verse 18)

SPEAKING OF THE FUTURE . . .

In the nineteenth century when schools taught children to read using the biblically based *McGuffey's Readers*, the prophet Daniel and his adventures in Babylon were common knowledge. Sadly, today such is no longer the case. The foundation and value of biblical prophecy has slipped precipitously near the edge of the cultural cliff. We know more about diets than we do about Daniel, more about fads than we do about the future, and more about profits than we do about prophets. And what a shame it is! For in addition to giving us confidence in the future, prophecy brings "edification and exhortation and comfort to men" (1 Corinthians 14:3).

When King Belshazzar arrayed himself in pompous pride before his guests at his great banquet (Daniel 5), the Aramaic words, "Mene, mene, tekel, upharsin" took shape on the wall before him. It took a prophet—those to whom God whispered His plans before revealing them to anyone else (Amos 3:7)—to step forward and translate Belshazzar's message of doom. Just as a personal prophecy foretold what would happen to King Belshazzar and his kingdom (he was killed that very night as the Persians invaded Babylon), so prophecy will tell us what to expect next in God's time table—if we pay attention.

We can read "the handwriting on the wall" today by paying attention to God's prophetic words recorded in the Bible.

SURELY THE LORD GOD DOES NOTHING, UNLESS HE REVEALS
HIS SECRET TO HIS SERVANTS THE PROPHETS.

—Amos in Amos 3:7

THE CHURCH OF SATAN'S CITY: PERGAMOS

Revelation 2:12-17

In this lesson we discover how easy it is for the world to enter the church.

You will find more in-depth information on this lesson in the book *Escape the Coming Night*, chapter 4, pages 61-65.

OUTLINE

Why are there so many different "churches" within Christianity? Where do different belief systems originate, and how? Why were so many different views allowed to develop? A study of a first-century church in Asia Minor reveals how compromise begins.

   I. **The Destination of the Letter**

  II. **The Designation of the Lord**

 III. **The Diagnosis of the Church**
     A. He Knew the Circumstances of Their Faith
     B. He Knew the Conviction of Their Faith
     C. He Knew the Courage of Their Faith
     D. He Knew the Compromise of Their Faith

 IV. **The Demand of the Church**

  V. **The Deliverance of the Church**
     A. The Hidden Manna
     B. The White Stone with a New Name

 VI. **The Problems of Pergamos Lived Out in History**

Many people wonder why there are so many different beliefs within Christendom. Comparing the clear teaching of the Word of God with developments in church history can help answer that question. In this lesson you may discover some things about "the church" that you did not know before, for example, how doctrines which are not found in the Bible have made their way into the doctrine and practice of the church. From the title of this lesson alone, "The Church of Satan's City," you get a forewarning of some of the unfortunate influences which can come to bear upon the church of Jesus Christ. Pergamos was the city that received the letter from Christ found in Revelation 2:12-17.

THE DESTINATION OF THE LETTER

Pergamos was the most northern of the seven cities and was the capital of the Roman government in Asia. It was considered the greatest city in Asia and had been the capital of Asia for almost 400 years when the letters of Revelation were written. Sir William Ramsay, who visited all of the cities of the churches in Revelation, said this about the city of Pergamos: "Beyond all other cities in Asia minor, it gives the traveler the impression of a royal city, the home of authority. The rocky hill on which it stands is so huge, and dominates the broad plain so proudly and so boldly."[1] The library of Pergamos was second only to the library at Alexandria, Egypt. So Pergamos was an intellectual center as well as a center of Roman authority and prominence.

THE DESIGNATION OF THE LORD (2:12)

When Christ introduces Himself to the church at Pergamos, He calls Himself "He who has the sharp two-edged sword," recalling the description in 1:16. The sword represents judgment, and Christ is prepared to use it in Pergamos if the church there does not repent (2:16). The Lord Jesus Christ, Judge of all the earth, is standing at the door of the church in Pergamos, the sword of His Word drawn, ready to speak words of diagnosis to them; He is going to tell them what they are doing

> *The Pergamum believers may have looked at each other and said, "What have we done?" They had become compromisers. Satan did not make a frontal attack by coming in as a roaring lion (1 Peter 5:8). He slithered in the back door and led them astray as a deceiving serpent.*
>
> *David Jeremiah*
> ***Escape the Coming Night***

wrong and how to repent of their actions and beliefs. The diagnosis
He gives them is four-fold—three good things and one that is bad.

THE DIAGNOSIS OF THE CHURCH (2:13)

If you receive a diagnosis from your doctor where three out of
the four conditions are good, you are thinking, "Three out of four
isn't bad. I must be in pretty good shape." But if the fourth condition
is life-threatening, then the three good things are cancelled out. That
was the problem with the church in Pergamos. Verse 13 contains the
initial diagnoses.

He Knew the Circumstances of Their Faith

The four-fold diagnosis begins with Christ telling the church in
Pergamos that He is aware of the difficulty of trying to hold firm to
the faith in the city where they live. He says He knows three things:
where they dwell, where Satan's throne is, and where Satan dwells.

The word for "stay" or "dwell" is a Greek word which means
"to have one's permanent address." Christ knows that the church is
locked into living in Satan's city, not a culture conducive to spiritual
growth. He knows the challenges that can present to believers. Rank
paganism radiated out from Pergamos all over Asia Minor. From a
Christian standpoint, it was probably the worst of the seven cities.
The references to Satan in Christ's words indicate how dark the
society was.

One of the ancient wonders of the world was the magnificent
altar to Zeus that was in Pergamos. It sat on the side of a mountain,
was 90 feet square and 40 feet high. Approaching the city from a
distance, the altar looked like a throne. On that altar many evil
sacrifices were offered, and scholars believe that is what Christ is
referring to when he mentions "Satan's throne" (2:13). Asclepius, the
god of healing, was known as the Pergamene God. The temples
of Asclepius were the nearest things to hospitals in the ancient
world. The temple of Asclepius was referred to as "Asclepius Soter," or
"Asclepius the Savior," which many believe was at the root of offense
which Christians took toward the whole city, that is, calling a pagan
god a "savior." An image of a snake coiled around a rod was the
emblem of Asclepius, an emblem still associated with doctors today.
So the association of a serpent with a pagan god called a "savior"
led to Pergamos being the dwelling place of Satan. (Another tradition
from history says that when Babylon fell, the center of Satan's
pagan activity on earth, he moved his operations from Babylon to
Pergamos.)

Christ was understanding of the darkness in which the
Christians in Pergamos were attempting to live. And He also knows

the difficult situations in which some believers today are trying to live and remain faithful to Him.

He Knew the Conviction of Their Faith

He knew that the believers were trying to "hold fast to [His] name" in Pergamos (2:13). Even though they were persecuted and threatened, they held fast to the faith. Pergamos was still orthodox as a church, and it had not surrendered one single doctrine of its faith.

He Knew the Courage of Their Faith

He also knew they had been courageous to the point of death; one of their members, Antipas, had died as a martyr. Even in the face of death they apparently were not giving up their beliefs nor denying the faith.

There is no record of this Antipas in books on secular or Christian history. Christ calls him "My faithful martyr," the word for martyr being the same as the word for "witness." In the ancient church being a faithful witness and being a martyr were almost one and the same thing. Many Christians today think of themselves as faithful witnesses, never having had their faith tested to the point of witnessing for Christ in death. Christ is referred to in Revelation as the "faithful witness" also (1:5; 3:14). When we are faithful to the Lord, we get the same name He has.

So far, so good. Christ knows the circumstances, conviction, and courage of their faith. The first three parts of their diagnosis are good. Unfortunately, the last part is the one that threatens their spiritual life.

He Knew the Compromise of Their Faith (2:14)

In each of the churches we have examined so far, Satan has had a different strategy to try to undermine the Church. Just as Satan knows our weaknesses and tries to trip us up accordingly, he knows the weakness of churches as well. His strategies are not random; rather, they are specific and calculated. Removing love for Christ was his strategy at Ephesus, and persecution by the Roman Empire was the strategy in Smyrna. In Pergamos he is going to try to weaken the church through compromise. The same strategy Balaam used against Israel was the strategy Satan brought against the church in Pergamos.

1. The doctrine of Balaam

   It's impossible to understand Revelation without knowing the Old Testament, in this case, Numbers 22-29. Balaam was a pagan prophet in the Old Testament who ran a business of getting the gods to grant favors. He would intercede with any god as long as the price was right. Balak, the king of Moab which was an enemy of Israel, wanted Israel destroyed. So he went to Balaam and offered to pay him to cause a curse to fall upon Israel. Balaam agreed, but try as he might he was unable to curse Israel. Every time he opened his mouth a blessing upon Israel came out. So Balaam taught Balak how to put a stumbling block in the path of Israel in the form of enticements from Moabite women. These women enticed Israelite men to take part in idolatrous sacrifices and commit sexual immorality (Numbers 25:1-3). In response, God killed 24,000 Israelites because they compromised their faith, because Balaam taught Balak how to make the Israelites stumble and fall.

The doctrine of Balaam is "If you cannot curse them, corrupt them." Balaam coveted money and was willing to do anything for it (2 Peter 2:15; Jude 11), including telling someone else how to lead them to sin. Christ brings the evil example of Balaam to light in the church at Pergamos. There were apparently some there who "[held] the doctrine of Balaam" (2:14), thinking they could indulge in the pagan practices around them without harm to their own spirituality. Though they had been courageous in maintaining their faith, they were beginning to compromise their faith by adding to it the practices of the pagans in Pergamos.

2. The doctrine of the Nicolaitans

We encountered a reference to the Nicolaitans in Ephesus (2:6). They were the ones who wanted to divide the church into two classes: the priests and the laity, just like the pagan temples. This was destroying the unity of the body of Christ. The idea of the clergy/laity divisions throughout church history had its beginning with the Nicolaitans.

The world was creeping into the church in Pergamos. Christ had diagnosed the problem and was ready to hold the church accountable.

> *The sin of Pergamum ... was the toleration of evil. Worldly standards had crept into their fellowship. Today it's the same worldly spirit within the church which makes it difficult to distinguish between the actions of Christians and the lifestyles of non-Christians. When those who call themselves Christians commit adultery, cheat in business, or lower their moral standards to suit the situation, they fit into the Pergamum mentality.*
>
> *David Jeremiah*
> ***Escape the Coming Night***

THE DEMAND OF THE CHURCH (2:16)

The Lord's words were simple: "Clean up this mess or I will come myself and fight against the guilty ones with the sword of My mouth." Roman officials had what was called "the right of the sword." But Christ said He had the true right to the sword and would exercise it if they did not repent.

THE DELIVERANCE OF THE CHURCH (2:17)

To the overcomers in the church at Pergamos, those who would separate themselves from the pagan practices in their community and in the church, Christ made two promises: hidden manna and a white stone with a new name.

The Hidden Manna

Manna, of course, was that heavenly food God gave the Israelites to keep them alive in the wilderness (Exodus 16:11-15). As a memorial to God's provision, a pot of manna was hidden away in the Ark of the Covenant in the tabernacle and later in the temple (Exodus 16:33-34; Hebrews 9:4). Christ is saying to the church that they cannot sit down at the table of pagans and eat that which has been sacrificed to idols. He has food for them which will sustain them and which only comes from heaven.

The White Stone with a New Name

This is the hardest symbol in the Book of Revelation to interpret. It was possibly representative of the white and black stones used in ancient courts by juries. A black stone meant guilty and a white stone meant innocent. Or it may have represented the amulets or charms that pagans carried for protection, upon which was inscribed the name of their god. You can see the application by comparison in either case. I could list a dozen more interpretations which have been suggested by scholars. Whatever is the correct view of the stone, the message from Christ was clear: You don't have to compromise your faith to get what you need.

THE PROBLEMS OF PERGAMOS LIVED OUT IN HISTORY

Ephesus represented the apostolic church and Smyrna the persecuted church. But Pergamos represents the church that got married to the world. This happened when Diocletian, the evil Roman Emperor, died and Constantine won control of the Empire. He decided the whole Empire should become Christian and declared it to be so. This unholy marriage of church and state resulted in Christianity being forced upon people, almost like emperor-worship had been. With all the official recognition of Christianity by Constantine there remains no evidence that he was a born again Christian.

Pagan temples became churches, pagan holidays became Christian holidays, pagan statues became Christian icons, and pagan priests slipped into positions of Christian influence. The marriage of church and state was underway, and the Pergamean period of church history was born. The world entered the church with the blessings of the emperor.

The warning for us today is never to bow the knee to anyone but Christ; never compromise our faith. We can do lots of good things for Christ, but bringing the world into the church can be the beginning of the end.

APPLICATION

1. Read 2 Corinthians 6:14-7:1.

a. What is the fundamental command Paul gives to the
Corinthians? (verse 14)

b. List the five questions Paul asks rhetorically to make his point.
(verses 14-16a)

1.

2.

3.

4.

5.

c. Whose temple are we as Christians? (verse 16)

d. How does Peter describe the church as the temple of God?
(1 Peter 2:4-5)

e. What does God expect us to do with regard to the pagan culture
around us? (verse 17)

f. If we "touch" that which is unclean, how does God respond?
(verse 17)

g. What were the believers at Pergamos doing that was unclean?

h. What are the chief temptations in our modern world for believers to "touch" that which is unclean and thereby compromise their faith?

i. If a father's children leave home to live with another family, how is that similar to spiritual adultery? (verse 18)

j. Where must we remain in order to receive the blessings of God's fatherhood?

k. What is Paul's summarizing exhortation? (verse 7:1)

l. What, if anything, is contaminating your "flesh and spirit" and keeping you from "perfecting holiness in the fear of God"?

2. Read Ephesians 4:3-6.

   a. If the body of Christ acts in a unified manner, what does that imply about what it believes?

   b. If we allow different beliefs to creep in, what will that do to unity?

   c. List all the "one's" that Paul mentions:

   d. List the "one's" that Jesus mentioned in Matthew 23:8-10:

e. What do you believe is the impact of disunity on our testimony to the world? (John 13:35)

SPEAKING OF THE FUTURE . . .

Over the last 2,000 years, many have labored to predict the time of Christ's return. Proponents of various predictions have rallied the faithful to quit their jobs, gather on mountain-tops, and await the sound of the heavenly trumpet splitting the night sky. So far, the dawns have filled their eyes with the sun rather than the Son.

We know it is fruitless to predict the time of His return. Jesus said that only His Father knows the day or the hour (Mark 13:32). He did tell a parable about a group of women who waited for the arrival of a bridegroom. Only the women who took enough oil to keep their lamps burning until the longer-than-expected arrival of the groom were invited into the wedding feast. The door was shut in the face of the rest. If that parable means anything, it means there is a connection between joy borne out of commitment and watchfulness, and regret borne out of carelessness. Keep your lamp trimmed—the marriage supper of the Lamb is one banquet you don't want to miss.

Those who look forward with anticipation to Christ's second coming are the ones who look back with gratitude to His first coming.

LOOKING FOR THE BLESSED HOPE AND GLORIOUS APPEARING OF OUR GREAT GOD AND SAVIOR JESUS CHRIST.

—Paul in Titus 2:13

Note:
[1] William Ramsay, *The Letters to the Seven Churches* (Grand Rapids: Baker Book House, 1963), 85.

THE ADULTEROUS CHURCH: THYATIRA

Revelation 2:18-29

In this lesson we discover the danger of tolerating immorality in an otherwise faithful church.

You will find more in-depth information on this lesson in the book *Escape the Coming Night*, chapter 4, pages 65-67.

OUTLINE

What defines a good church? Surely such a definition would include ministry to others, love, loyalty, patience, and progress in spiritual growth. But would it also include toleration of a known sexually immoral person? No, as Jesus makes perfectly clear.

I. **The Destination of the Letter**

II. **The Designation of the Lord**
    A. His Designation as the Son of God
    B. His Designation as the All-Seeing God
    C. His Designation as the One with Feet Like Fine Brass

III. **The Diagnosis of the Church**
    A. Thyatira Was a Laboring Church
    B. Thyatira Was a Loving Church
    C. Thyatira Was a Loyal Church
    D. Thyatira Was a Longsuffering Church
    E. Thyatira Was a Maturing, Progressing, Growing Church

IV. **The Denunciation of the Church**

V. **The Declaration to the Church**
    A. The Message to the Cult
    B. The Message to the Christians
    C. The Message to the Conquerors

I n all the churches we have studied up to this point a similar pattern has emerged: genuinely commendable qualities marred by carelessness in one particular area. And that area of spiritual carelessness has the effect of making powerless the other positive qualities. The church at Thyatira worked hard, loved faithfully, was loyal in service, and had great faith and patience. But there was a chink in her spiritual armor which caught the attention of Jesus, the Head of the Church. The message of repentance comes to yet another of the churches in Asia Minor, and continues to the church of today. Revelation 2:18-29 reveals the problem in Thyatira.

THE DESTINATION OF THE LETTER

Unlike some of the other cities Jesus addresses, Thyatira was not known for its grandeur, its culture, or its learning. But it was known for its commerce. It was located in a valley between two cities on one of the busiest trade routes running through Asia Minor. The city boasted numerous trade guilds—bakers, bronze workers, clothiers, cobblers, weavers, tanners, dyers, potters, and others. All had guilds, or unions, in Thyatira to protect their workers and promote their trade. Though Thyatira seems to have been the least important of the seven cities, she receives the longest of the seven letters of Christ.

THE DESIGNATION OF THE LORD (2:18)

Picking up some of the descriptive elements of Christ from the first chapter, the Lord is here introduced in a number of ways.

His Designation as the Son of God

It is important to note that Jesus introduces Himself as the Son of God. When we are introduced shortly to a woman who acts like a reincarnation of the infamous Jezebel of the Old Testament, who considered herself to be a prophetess of God, it will be important to remember that the Son of God stands in judgment over the prophet or prophetess of God. The authority of Christ is established first.

His Designation as the All-Seeing God

Second, Jesus calls Himself one "who has eyes like a flame of fire." The point of eyes being like fire is that nothing can stand before fire. It destroys everything it comes in contact with so that nothing remains hidden. Eyes of fire means that Christ sees all; nothing can be kept from the searching gaze of His sight.

God's knowledge of all things is mentioned often in Scripture. He saw Hagar alone in the wilderness (Genesis 16:13), and Jeremiah knew God tests the hearts and mind of all men (Jeremiah 11:20). The apostles knew as well (Acts 1:24; 15:8). John the apostle tells us that Jesus knew what was in all men (John 2:24-25). Knowing what was happening in the church at Thyatira was consistent with eyes that see all things.

His Designation as the One with Feet Like Fine Brass

We learned at the beginning of these lessons that brass in Scripture is always an indication of judgment. God tells Israel that when they sin the "heavens which are over your head shall be bronze [brass]," meaning their prayers will go unheard and the blessing of rain will be stopped (Deuteronomy 28:23). That judgment is spelled out in no uncertain terms in 2:23, whereupon all the churches will know who is searching the hearts and minds of believers everywhere.

There is nothing more piercing than flaming fire. Everything yields and melts before it. It penetrates all things, consumes every opposition, sweeps down all obstructions, and presses its way with invincible power. And of this sort are the eyes of Jesus. They look through everything; they pierce through all masks and coverings; they search the remotest recesses; they behold the most hidden things of the soul; and there is no escape from them.

Joseph Seiss

It is important for the church today to realize that the Christ who stood ready to judge the seven churches in Revelation stands ready to judge our churches today. What has changed except the passage of time? Nothing. The resurrected Christ searching the hearts of His people in the first century is also searching the hearts of His people in the 21st century. And He will also judge His church with perfect knowledge at the Judgment Seat of Christ someday. That reality gives me cold chills when I think of it. Christ is our loving and compassionate Savior and friend, but He is also our judge as well.

THE DIAGNOSIS OF THE CHURCH (2:19)

The compassion of the Lord is seen as He speaks first to the church of their positive characteristics, those things with which He is pleased in their lives.

Thyatira Was a Laboring Church

First is mentioned the church's works, which is a general reference to their good deeds. But then the more specific term "service" is mentioned. This means they were involved in ministry to others. The word for "service" is the same word from which the word "deacons" comes, a word that means to serve. More than just a specific function or job, the reference is to their unofficial, non-mandatory acts of kindness to all people. The fact that they were a laboring, ministering church was pleasing to Jesus.

Thyatira Was a Loving Church

Even with the significant moral errors He was about to reveal to them, the church at Thyatira was still a church which exercised love. As Paul said in 1 Corinthians, chapter 13, the greatest of the virtues is love, and the church at Thyatira exercised that virtue with nobility. It is interesting to recall that the church at Ephesus wouldn't tolerate false teachers or apostles, but at the same time they had lost their heart of love for Christ, and therefore for others. The church at Thyatira was the opposite; they had love but lacked discernment. Some churches are strong in one way while other churches are weak in the same area. Jesus points out the strengths of both and the weaknesses of both.

Thyatira Was a Loyal Church

Jesus commends their faith, expressed by the Greek word *pistis,* meaning faithfulness, fidelity, or loyalty. The saints at Thyatira were dependable and reliable. Some Christians run well at the outset of the race, but after they go for a while and the pressure is on, they drop out. However, the church at Thyatira was loyal.

Thyatira Was a Longsuffering Church

Patience was next on Jesus' list of commendable traits of the Thyatirans. Patience is the ability to be still when everything around us is storm-tossed. Patience is from *hupomone,* a word which means "to abide or remain under." Patience stays where it is, under the most difficult circumstances. It doesn't flee or quit or give up. Just as the Christians in Smyrna would not quit when they were persecuted, so the Thyatirans would not quit. They were a patient people.

Thyatira Was a Maturing, Progressing, Growing Church

There was a fifth characteristic which is less specific than the other four; indeed, it serves as sort of an umbrella under which all their positive traits fit. Their more recent works, Jesus said, are more than the first. In other words, this was a church that was maturing and progressing and growing—a church making progress in sanctification. They were more loyal, more loving, more patient, more serving than when they first began.

While this was a commendable church in many respects, that in which they were failing overshadowed all the good they were doing.

THE DENUNCIATION OF THE CHURCH (2:20)

Verse 20 begins like a conversation you have with your boss in which all of your good points are highlighted. Then comes the, "But . . . ." I hope you never hear anything said to you as harsh as what Jesus said to the church at Thyatira: "You allow that woman Jezebel, who calls herself a prophetess, to teach and seduce My servants to commit sexual immorality and eat things sacrificed to idols." There was a cancer in the body, a weed in the garden, in Thyatira. The devil's strategy was to introduce evil into the church through a woman who promoted sexual immorality.

The original Jezebel was the wife of the wicked king of Israel, Ahab. Her father was a priest of Ashtaroth, the Phoenician equivalent of the Greek Aphrodite and the Roman Venus. Under these gods religion was divorced from morality and sexual immorality was actually made a part of "worship." Therefore, a priestess in the worship of Ashtaroth was nothing more than a prostitute. Ahab never should have married a woman such as Jezebel. She brought all her wicked religious background into the kingdom of Israel. She persuaded Ahab to build a temple to Ashtaroth in Samaria (1 Kings 16:30-31), supported 850 prophets of her immoral cult, and began systematically killing the prophets of God (1 Kings 19:2). She must have been a fearsome woman since Elijah ran for his life from her. She was the epitome of corruption, immorality, and idolatry.

The original Jezebel had been dead a thousand years, but there apparently was a woman in the church at Thyatira who was promoting the same licentious and immoral lifestyle, claiming to be a prophetess. Idolatry leading to immorality is always the pattern that surfaces, and it gets worse over time. Ephesus couldn't tolerate false teaching. Pergamos had some who practiced the doctrines of Balaam and the Nicolaitans. And Thyatira "allowed" (2:20) an immoral woman in their midst. Total rejection in Ephesus became toleration in Thyatira. Jesus is about to make three declarations to address a serious sin problem in the church at Thyatira.

> *If the devil cannot conquer the church by the application of political pressure or the propagation of intellectual heresy, he will try the insinuation of moral evil. This was the dragon's strategy in Thyatira.*
>
> *John Stott*

THE DECLARATION TO THE CHURCH (2:21-25)

The Jezebel cult gets the first message, then the Christians not involved with the cult. Finally, those who purpose to live above immorality, those who are conquerors, hear from Him.

The Message to the Cult (2:21-23)

Those involved in the Jezebel cult had been given time to repent, but apparently they (or she, the leader) had not done so. A terrible judgment is therefore pronounced upon her. She will be cast into a bed of affliction (of sickness) and those who had followed her would be cast into tribulation. I wonder if the old adage, "You've made your own bed; now you have to sleep in it," came from the judgment levied against her. Not only will she suffer, and those who have followed her, but her children will suffer as well, indeed, they will be killed. All of this judgment will take place in a way that all the churches will know that Christ is the one who searches the mind and heart of believers, that He is in charge.

The church at Thyatira represents the church of Jesus Christ during the Middle (Dark) Ages. During that period the church accomplished little for God because it sought to combine Christianity with pagan philosophy and heathen religious practice. Religious syncretism is unholy in God's sight whether in the first century, the 13th century, or the 21st century.

The Message to the Christians (2:24-25)

There were Christians in the church who did not follow after Jezebel, and Jesus spares them from any additional burden. This situation is similar to the first church conference held in Jerusalem to decide how to handle the transition of Jews into Christianity, the body of Christ (Acts 15). They decided on a minimum set of standards for Gentile believers to keep from giving offense to the transitioning Jewish believers, and laid no additional burdens on them in terms of rules or regulations. Keep it simple, the leaders were saying, and that seems to be what Jesus is saying as well. In a day when we tend to multiply rules upon rules in the body of Christ, Jesus just said, "Keep doing what you're doing—not following the Jezebel woman." Just serve God and keep doing what you're doing.

The Message to the Conquerors (2:26-29)

Finally, there is a message to the overcomers. He makes two promises to them. First, if they will stay faithful to Him, they will be given the right to rule one day. This is a reference to the day when the saints of God will rule and reign with Christ. Second, there is the promise of the Rapture of the church. The "morning star" (2:28) seems to be a reference to Christ as the One who will come in the dark hour preceding the dawn of the kingdom of God (the Millennium). Christ is the "bright and morning star" (Revelation 22:16). To be raptured with Christ only to return to rule with Him makes being faithful a rewarding decision.

The message to the church at Thyatira is to repent if you are involved in immorality and continue overcoming if you are not involved. In a day ripe with immorality, that message of Christ applies to the church with renewed urgency. "He who has an ear, let him hear what the Spirit says to the churches" (Revelation 2:29).

APPLICATION

1. What do you discover about the Old Testament Jezebel's character and influence from the following passages of Scripture?

   a. 1 Kings 16:29-33

   b. 1 Kings 18:4, 13, 19

   c. 1 Kings 19:1-3

   d. 1 Kings 21:1-16

   e. 2 Kings 9:22

2. Read 1 Corinthians 5:1-13.

   a. What problem was Paul addressing in the church at Corinth? (verse 1)

   b. What fact does Paul mention that made this problem particularly shameful in the community? (verse 1)

   c. Why were the Corinthians "puffed up," or proud, over their tolerance? (verse 2)

   d. What should their attitude have been instead of pride in their "liberty" and attitude of acceptance? (verse 2)

   e. How did Paul's attitude resemble that of Christ toward immorality in the church? Was it grace or judgment? (verse 3)

f. What were they to do with the immoral person? (verses 5, 13)

g. Why must immorality be dealt with quickly in the church? (verses 6-8)

h. Why does Paul draw a distinction between associating with sexually immoral people in the church and outside the church? (verses 9-10)

i. What should our attitude be toward a Christian who practices immorality? (verse 11)

j. What should be our first responsibility—immorality in the culture or in the church? (verses 12-13)

SPEAKING OF THE FUTURE . . .

When I (David Jeremiah) was a teenager, my parents left for a trip, leaving me home alone. I was mature enough, they thought, to look after things and to stay out of trouble. Well, I didn't get into trouble, but neither did I "look after things" the way I should have. I let the dishes and laundry pile up and didn't do any cleaning or housework.

Though I knew they'd be gone several days, I didn't know the exact date of their return—I only knew it would be within a certain window of time. As a result, I got the house cleaned and took care of all my jobs by the beginning of that window. I didn't know when they would arrive, but I wanted to be ready when they did.

Jesus Christ is going to return to earth. We don't know the exact day or time, but there is good reason to believe, biblically speaking, that it could be soon. There are certain tasks He has left for us to fulfill in His absence: spreading the Gospel, making disciples, and perfecting our own holiness. The fact that Christ will return soon should prompt us to be about those tasks with alertness, readiness, and faithfulness.

Those who most anticipate the return of Jesus are those who have been most obedient to Jesus.

> AND NOW, LITTLE CHILDREN, ABIDE IN HIM,
> THAT WHEN HE APPEARS, WE MAY HAVE CONFIDENCE AND
> NOT BE ASHAMED BEFORE HIM AT HIS COMING.
>
> —John in 1 John 2:28

THE DEAD CHURCH: SARDIS

Revelation 3:1-6

In this lesson we discover why churches die.

You will find more in-depth information on this lesson in the book *Escape the Coming Night*, chapter 4, pages 67-71.

OUTLINE

Some churches resemble mausoleums, pretty and well-kept on the outside, but devoid of life on the inside. Why do churches die? Most of the reasons people give are wrong. When any living body dies, it is only because the individual cells began dying long before the end came.

I. **The Destination of the Letter**

II. **The Designation of the Lord**

III. **The Denunciation of the Church**
   A. The Church Is Denounced for Its Outward Profession and Inward Deadness
   B. The Church Is Denounced for Its Incomplete Works

IV. **The Direction to the Church**
   A. Become Vigilant
   B. Become Vigorous
   C. Become Victorious
   D. Become Vibrant
   E. Become Virtuous

V. **The Declaration to the Church**
   A. To Those Who Are Overcoming, They Shall Be Clothed in White
   B. To Those Who Are Overcoming, They Shall Be Continued in the Book
   C. To Those Who Are Overcoming, They Shall Be Confessed Before the Father

VI. **How Does a Church Die?**
   A. What We Can Rule Out
   B. What Causes Death

The city of Sardis was considered to be one of the most impregnable cities of its day. Situated fifteen hundred feet above the valley floor on the top of a mountain spur, it was surrounded by sheer cliffs on three sides and a narrow isthmus on the fourth. The greatest king of Sardis was named Croesus, a man remembered for his great wealth. Unfortunately, it was his overconfidence in the security of his city that caused its downfall.

Croesus, against better advice, went to war against Cyrus, king of Persia. He was defeated and driven back into his city where he felt he was totally safe. Cyrus offered a reward to any of his soldiers who could figure out a way into the fortress of Sardis. By chance, a Persian soldier noticed a Sardinian soldier drop his helmet accidentally over the city wall. When the Sardinian appeared briefly at the bottom of the wall to retrieve his helmet, the Persian soldier knew there had to be a passageway into the city. Under cover of darkness, a Persian raiding party found the opening, made their way into the city and opened the gates from the inside. The Sardinians had no guard posted, so confident were they in the strength of their fortress. After that defeat, Sardis was defeated a century later in almost the same way. Twice, the city was destroyed because of overconfidence in its own security.

THE DESTINATION OF THE LETTER

The fifth letter of Christ to the churches was sent to the church at Sardis. Many figures from secular history are associated with Sardis, including the Greek philosopher Thales and the Athenian legislator Solon. Further, it is remembered as the first center for the minting of gold and silver coins. More than anything, it is remembered as the city defeated by a surprise attack, a piece of history which may have prompted Jesus' admonition to the church to be watchful (3:3).

THE DESIGNATION OF THE LORD (3:1)

Our Lord writes this letter to the church in Sardis, and He designates Himself this way: "These things says He who has the seven Spirits of God and the seven stars" (verse 1). In an earlier lesson we mentioned the seven Spirits of God as referring to the Holy Spirit in His fullness. There were seven churches and a seven-fold ministry and presence of the Spirit. The Holy Spirit was active in all seven of the churches to which Christ wrote letters. The seven stars refer to the angels (or ministers, or pastors) of the seven churches (1:20). So Jesus is saying to the church in Sardis that He has the Holy Spirit and control over the pastors of the seven churches.

THE DENUNCIATION OF THE CHURCH (3:1-2)

Unlike previous letters, this letter begins with a sharp denunciation of the church: "You have a name that you are alive, but you are dead."

The Church Is Denounced for Its Outward Profession and Inward Deadness

Sardis may have been the birthplace of the "nominal Christian" in Christendom, a person who is a Christian in name only. Sardis was apparently filled with people like that. The church at Sardis was more of a mausoleum than a church, a well-kept place filled with dead men's bones.

Nominal belief is critiqued often in Scripture. Isaiah the prophet spoke for the Lord on one occasion pointing out people who drew near with their mouths and lips but whose hearts were from the Lord (Isaiah 29:13). On the outside things look great, but the Lord who has eyes of flaming fire can see inside the heart and know what its condition really is. Jesus spoke to the Pharisees about their nominal faith. The Pharisees gave money, said prayers, and fasted, and did it all publicly so people would be impressed. But in Matthew 23 Jesus called them hypocrites, whitewashed tombs full of uncleanness on the inside. Outwardly they appeared righteous but inwardly they were full of hypocrisy and lawlessness (Matthew 23:27).

The Church Is Denounced for Its Incomplete Works

Christ says, "I have not found your works perfect before God." The word "perfect" in the text is the word "finished, complete, or fulfilled." The Christians in Sardis were physically alive but spiritually dead, and there was nothing going on that had been completed. It was like religion that never got past the infant stage, never grew to maturity in Christ.

> *We can have a fine choir, and expensive organ, good music, great anthems and fine congregational singing. We can mouth hymns and psalms with unimpeachable elegance, while our mind wanders and our heart is far from God. We can have pomp and ceremony, color and ritual, liturgical exactness and ecclesiastical splendor, and yet be offering a worship which is not perfect or "fulfilled" in the sight of God.*
>
> *John Stott*

And so our Lord, on the basis of His denunciation, gives some strong words of instruction to the church.

THE DIRECTION TO THE CHURCH (3:2-3)

In the church at Sardis there were three groups of people: unsaved people, carnal Christians (who acted like they were unsaved), and a remnant of Christians who loved God and were trying to make the church what it should have been. Although Jesus was writing to the church as a whole, we can pick out words He addresses to each of the three groups.

Become Vigilant

Jesus is saying to the church, "You are about ready to lose everything you have. In My eyes, I have already seen that you are dead. There is a little bit left, but you are going to lose it all if you don't wake up, if you don't become vigilant." In Paul's letter to the Ephesians, he said something similar: "Awake, you who sleep, Arise from the dead" (Ephesians 5:14).

I occasionally have people question the need for membership in the local church, suggesting that we let anyone who wants to "join" just do so by their attendance and involvement. But church membership, and the examination processes which accompany it, is an attempt to keep a good church from going bad over time. It is a way to keep the focus on the truth and on spiritual life so that false teaching or sin doesn't creep in unawares.

Become Vigorous

Those who are true believers in the church must be vigorous in strengthening the remnant that remains. At Sardis there were a "few" who had not "defiled their garments" (3:4), and they needed to be strengthened and built up. I have met many people who attend a small church where perhaps generations of their family have attended, and they struggle along with a handful of others to keep it alive through a small Bible study or whatever they can do. However, the leadership is "dead" and the church is almost that way. But God throughout history has always had a remnant, a few in whom the light of truth remained alive.

Become Victorious

Physical death in a person is the separation of the spirit from the body—and the same is true in the death of a church. When the Spirit of God leaves the body of Christ in a particular church, that church dies. When Jesus tells the church at Sardis to "remember therefore how you have received and heard," I believe it is a veiled reference to the Holy Spirit and His ministry in the church. When we are born again we receive the gift of the Holy Spirit and we hear the teaching of the truth. A church full of people who are full of the Holy Spirit will be a church that is full of the Holy Spirit. To the degree the Spirit is never invited into the lives of church members, to that degree the church begins to die. And over time, a church is more dead than alive—which was true of the church at Sardis. They needed to regain the victory they had when all their members were filled with the Spirit.

Become Vibrant

The next phrase is, "hold fast . . ." (verse 3:3). Usually in Scripture that admonition is given with reference to doctrine and belief (1 Corinthians 15:2; 1 Thessalonians 5:21; 2 Timothy 1:13; Hebrews 4:14; 10:23). So Jesus says to this church that, if they have any hope of living again, they must hold fast to the truth, and thereby have a vibrant faith and belief.

Become Virtuous

The command to "repent" is a command to restore virtue. God wants the church to be clean, pure, and holy. Because there were only a "few" who had not "defiled their garments," what does that say about the many? Most had lost their spiritual and moral virtue, and thus needed to repent. Christ declares to the church three ways by which, if they repent, they could become overcomers and restore life to their church.

THE DECLARATION TO THE CHURCH (3:5-6)

To Those Who Are Overcoming, They Shall Be Clothed in White

Being clothed in white signifies righteousness. Overcomers will clothe themselves in righteousness so as not to defile themselves. In heaven the church will be clothed in "the righteous acts of the saints" (Revelation 19:8). For many believers that would come close to indecent exposure! True overcomers will be brilliant in the whiteness of righteousness.

To Those Who Are Overcoming, They Shall Be Continued in the Book

Ancient cities kept registers of all their citizens. If a citizen was convicted of a crime, not only was he punished but his name was blotted out of the city registry. Or, if he performed some heroic feat, his name would be embellished with gold letters. Overcomers' names will never be removed from the Book of Life.

To Those Who Are Overcoming, They Shall Be Confessed Before the Father

The Bible says if we confess Jesus before men He will confess us before the Father (Matthew 10:32). This is the last phase of the promises Jesus makes to those who overcome the temptations to fall away or just be a nominal Christian. We will be clothed in righteousness, our names will be in the Book of Life, and we will be confessed before the Father.

HOW DOES A CHURCH DIE?

We can rule out some things to start with:

What We Can Rule Out

1. We may rule out death from an outside enemy.

   History shows it is almost impossible to kill the church externally. The church at Sardis did not die from persecution. Persecution normally makes the church grow and get stronger.

2. We may rule out death by suicide.

   There was no conscious break with Christ; they didn't take a vote and decide to pronounce the benediction over their church and bury it. I've never heard of a church doing that.

3. We may rule out death by abandonment.

   The church wasn't abandoned by God. We know that because there was still a remnant there. God was still willing for the church to be alive and grow if the people were.

What Causes Death

The truth about this is frightening to consider, but every Christian needs to hear it.

1. The church died through the death of its individual members.

   A church is like a human body and its individual cells, its overall health, is only as good as the health of each cell. A church is nothing except the composite assembly of its individual members. When the members of a church die, the church ultimately dies.

> A church is in danger of death when it begins to worship its own past...when it is more concerned with forms than with life...when it loves systems more than it loves Jesus Christ...when it is more concerned with material than spiritual things.
>
> William Ramsay

2. The church died from relying on its past reputation.

   Sardis isn't the only church to have lived on its laurels. But you can only do that for so long before death sets in. Vance Havner used to say that spiritual movements go through four stages: a man, a movement, a machine, and a monument. The church at Sardis had become a monument; anything that happened spiritually had happened in the past. The church died the same way the city died, from overconfidence and a lack of vigilance.

3. The church died because it was not sensitive to its own spiritual condition.

   The church at Sardis was not even conscious of its own death. They were still going through the motions. They had lulled themselves to sleep over the years and didn't even realize they had died. They were like Samson in the Old Testament who "did not know that the LORD had departed from him" (Judges 16:20).

Christians don't lose their salvation, but their lives can so grieve the Holy Spirit that there is no life, no power, no vibrancy in their lives. And when most of the people in a church do that, then there is no life in the church. They have become dead to the things of the Lord. Every Christian should look at his own life as a barometer of the life of his church. As the members go, so eventually will go the church.

APPLICATION

1. Read Matthew 23:1-39.

   a. What was the sure sign that the Pharisees were hypocrites? (verse 3b)

   b. Who were their works done for? (verse 5)

   c. What did they do to call attention to themselves? (verses 5b-7)

   d. What is the warning statement of Scripture about man-centered, nominal religion? (verse 12)

   e. List the seven "Woe's," and their meaning, given by Jesus to the Pharisees:

   1) 23:13-14

   2) 23:15

   3) 23:16-22

   4) 23:23-24

   5) 23:25-26

   6) 23:27-28

7) 23:29-32

f. How does the warning given to the Pharisees compare to the warnings given to the church at Sardis? (verses 33-37)

g. What was Jerusalem's response to the plea of Christ to turn to the Lord? (verse 37b)

h. Compare Matthew 23:38 with a "dying church" such as the church at Sardis.

i. What was the sure sign that the Pharisees were not aware of their own spiritual "death"? (Luke 11:53-54)

2. What does God always preserve for Himself even in times of spiritual deadness? (Romans 9:27; 11:5)

a. How does a person who is part of God's remnant know that he is?

b. Would a person who was not a part of the remnant (a person who was a nominal Christian) believe he was not?

c. What should the remnant do in a near-dead local church to overcome the impact and effect of the lack of spiritual life?

d. Are you part of the remnant in your church? How do you know?

SPEAKING OF THE FUTURE . . .

Since America's entrance into combat in Afghanistan and Iraq in 2003, we have heard a constant stream of debate, discussion, and dialogue about the decision to go to war. Not only have we heard the president and others justifying America's actions, we have heard from those opposed. At the beginning of the war in Iraq, television news footage showed massive demonstrations all around the world against the war. The avocation of activism is alive and well, as it should be, in democracies everywhere.

The right to speak one's mind is a cherished privilege of freedom. Far too often, however, activists raise their voices and carry their signs in opposition to something. We know what they are against, but sometimes have difficulty determining what they are for. In a day when life for most people is a puzzle, when the confusion of chaos reigns, we need to know how to sort the pieces out for those looking for answers.

So I am for Christian activism, but of a different sort. I believe we need to "take to the streets" of the world and declare the Bible's answers to the chaotic times in which we live—the answers found in Bible prophecy. Life doesn't have to be an unsolvable puzzle. Taking the pieces of God's end-time prophecies out of the box and constructing them according to His already-painted picture will give us the answers we need in difficult times.

> YOU KNOW HOW TO DISCERN THE FACE OF THE SKY,
> BUT YOU CANNOT DISCERN THE SIGNS OF THE TIMES.
>
> —Jesus in Matthew 16:3

THE FAITHFUL CHURCH: PHILADELPHIA

Revelation 3:7-13

In this lesson we see the effects of the largest army in history.

You will find more in-depth information on this lesson in the book *Escape the Coming Night*, chapter 4, pages 71-74.

OUTLINE

It is possible to be part of a church with which the Lord Jesus is pleased. But what kind of church is it? Is it one measured by the size of buildings, member rolls, or financial giving? Jesus commended the church at Philadelphia, but not for meeting our modern standards of success.

I. **The Destination of the Letter**

II. **The Designation of the Lord**

III. **The Diagnosis of the Lord**
   A. They Have an Open Door
   B. They Have a Little Strength
   C. They Have Kept the Word of God
   D. They Have Not Denied the Lord

IV. **The Declaration of Christ to the Church**
   A. He Promises to Humiliate Their Enemies
   B. He Promises to Keep Them from the Hour of Trial
   C. He Promises to Come Quickly

V. **The Direction for Us**

We come in this lesson to the church where I would have most wanted to be on the day the mailman delivered the letters from the Lord. I would not have wanted to identify with or be a member of some of the other churches. But the church of Philadelphia received a letter with encouraging words from Jesus Christ, words which would have been a great motivation and represented a great opportunity for continued ministry for the Lord. Philadelphia, the church of brotherly love, received commendation appropriate for a church of overcomers.

THE DESTINATION OF THE LETTER

The word *philadelphia* is almost identical to the city we know by the same name, Philadelphia, and means "brotherly love." The noun and adjective forms of the word occur seven times in the New Testament besides its use as a city name (Revelation 1:11; 3:7). It is normally translated as "kindly affectionate" or "brotherly love" (Romans 12:10; 1 Thessalonians 4:9; Hebrews 13:1; 1 Peter 1:22; 3:8; 2 Peter 1:7).

From the perspective of church history, the church at Philadelphia represents the period from the beginning of the 19th century to the Rapture of the Church, what we might call the "revived" church—the period following the Reformation. It was a time of great missionary outreach, revivals, and the advent of the Christian education movement. It is the Philadelphian church which will be in existence in some form when Christ returns for His own.

THE DESIGNATION OF THE LORD (3:7)

When the Lord writes to the church in Philadelphia, he gives to Himself these characteristics: holy, true, having the key of David, able to open and shut according to His will (3:7). He positions Himself as the preeminent, holy God, alone qualified to call the Christians of Philadelphia to a life of faith in Him. Because He is holy, He can call us to be holy (1 Peter 1:15).

The reference to His being true is a reference to His genuineness or reality; He is the real thing, the essence of deity. He is true and holy, the perfect combination of doctrine and pure living. Not only is He characterized by that combination, He wants us to share in both of those characteristics as well. The reference to Him having the key of David thrusts us back into the Old Testament. In the prior description of Christ in chapter one He had the keys of Hades and of Death (1:18). But here it is the key of David. This is a reference to Isaiah 22:22, where speaking of Eliakim it is recorded that, "The key of the house of David I will lay on his shoulder; So he shall open,

and no one shall shut; And he shall shut, and no one shall open."
Eliakim had the key to all of the treasures of the king, and when
he opened the door, it was open. And when he closed the door, it
was closed.

Christ is pictured here as the anti-type of Eliakim. He has the
key to truth and holiness as well as the key to opportunity and
service for a church surrounded by heathenism and wickedness.
When He opens the door to truth and ministry no one can shut it.

THE DIAGNOSIS OF THE LORD

It is fitting that the one who holds the key proceeds to tell the
church that they have an open door before them.

They Have an Open Door (3:8)

When He tells the church in Philadelphia they have an open door, it could mean several things. We have our best clue in 1 Corinthians 16:8-9 where Paul refers to an "effective door" which has opened to him for ministry. In 2 Corinthians 2:12 he refers to another open door in Troas, meaning an opportunity for ministry God set before him. In Colossians 4:3 Paul requests prayer for a "door for the word" to open, referring again to a testimony to preach the Gospel. So an open door in Scripture is an opportunity for ministry God sets before us.

Philadelphia was situated at a "corner" where three regions came together: Lycia, Lydia, and Phrygia. The city was founded in 140 B.C. by Philadelphus, the king of Pergamos. The city was founded there so it might be a gateway for the spread of Hellenism (Greek language and customs) into the surrounding regions. Philadelphia was the key,

> Christ has the keys and He opens the doors. Then let us not barge our way unceremoniously through doors which are still closed. We must wait for Him to make openings for us. Damage is continually being done to the cause of Christ by rude or blatant testimony. It is indeed right to seek to win for Christ our friends and relatives at home and at work, but we are sometimes in a greater hurry than God is. Be patient, pray hard, love much, and wait expectantly for the opportunity of witness. The same applies to our future. More mistakes are probably made by speed than by sloth, by impatience than by deleteriousness. God's purposes often ripen slowly and if the door is shut, don't put your shoulder to it. Wait till Christ takes out the key and opens it up.
>
> John Stott

the gateway, to the central part of Asia Minor. So when Jesus spoke to the Philadelphians of a wide-open door, they would have immediately thought of the history of their city and the opportunity to influence thousands of people. But now the door is open for influence of a different kind. It is easy to see the comparison of the Philadelphia church with the period of history I described earlier when so many ministry opportunities opened for spreading the Gospel.

They Have a Little Strength

This second commendation sounds like a backhanded compliment: "You have a little strength." The meaning here is not that the church "still" has a little strength left by which they can function. Rather it means that they "only" have a little strength. Therefore, their strength will have to come from another source. As Paul said in 2 Corinthians 12:9, his power was made perfect in weakness. If the Lord is the one opening the door, then He will provide the strength to walk through it.

They Have Kept the Word of God

The third commendation is that they had kept God's Word. In the midst of a pagan region of the world, the church at Philadelphia believed the Word of God and remained faithful to it.

They Have Not Denied the Lord

Finally, they did not deny the name of the Lord Jesus Christ. There was much controversy toward the end of the apostolic age about the deity of Christ. But the church at Philadelphia stood strong in their belief in who Jesus was—God in the flesh, the Lord and Savior of mankind.

Many church growth experts have identified the four characteristics of the Philadelphia church as characteristics of growing congregations: identification of open doors for ministry, dependence upon the Lord for strength, commitment to the Word, and submission to the Lordship of Christ.

THE DECLARATION OF CHRIST TO THE CHURCH (3:9-13)

He Promises to Humiliate Their Enemies

Once again we encounter the trouble-making Jews of the "synagogue of Satan." They were part of the church but continued to cause trouble of a theological and practical nature. They were mentioned in the letter to the church at Smyrna in a more tolerant tone, but here there is a more strident tone taken by the Lord toward them: "I will make them come and worship before your feet, and know that I have loved you." Just as the Lord humbled the Apostle Paul and caused him to join those who worshipped the One he was against, so the Lord will cause these Jews to be humbled before the faithful at Philadelphia.

He Promises to Keep Them from the Hour of Trial

The next promise Christ makes to the church has great prophetic significance. In verse 10 He tells the church He will keep them from the hour of trial that is coming upon the whole world. Note this is not referring to a regional persecution; it is a time of testing that will come upon the whole world. Note secondly that this is not a time of testing through which they will pass but be kept safe. Rather, it is a promise that they, and the church in history represented by the Philadelphian church, will be kept from ever experiencing the tribulation coming upon the earth (described in Revelation 4-19).

This promise to the Philadelphia church has great importance as far as how one views the Tribulation period to which it makes reference. There are three views regarding the Tribulation held in the church. One is that the church is raptured before it begins and so avoids the entire seven year period. Another is that the church is raptured mid-way through the Tribulation. And the third is that the church endures the Tribulation and is protected through it, and then is raptured when it is over. These are the Pre-Tribulation, Mid-Tribulation, and Post-Tribulation views of the Rapture of the church.

The "hour of trial" Jesus refers to is the Tribulation. Some people believe that the church will go through the Tribulation like Shadrach, Meshach, and Abednego went through the trial of the fiery furnace without harm. But Jesus didn't say He would keep the church "through" the hour of trial, He said "from" the hour of trial. The church will be no where near the Tribulation when it starts because Jesus will call us from the realm of that trouble, the earth, to Himself.

It is interesting that the word "church" is found 19 times in the first three chapters of Revelation. But from Revelation 4 on, which describes the Tribulation, there is no further reference to the church on earth. It would seem logical that if we were going to be going through this awful time on earth that the Lord would have included some reference to it in Revelation 4-19. The reason for silence regarding the church is that we are in heaven during that time of testing.

Another indication that the church is in heaven is found with the 24 seats around the throne of God mentioned in Revelation, chapter four. Most believe those 24 elders represent the church which is in heaven as the Tribulation begins on earth. And think of this: If the church was destined to go through the awfulness of the Tribulation period, wouldn't you rather die and go to be with the Lord now than to go through such a horrible time? The reality is that God is not going to divide His body, part of it in heaven and part on earth during the Tribulation. All of Christ's body will be united with Him during those days.

Finally, there are two additional reasons for Christ taking the church to heaven during the Tribulation. First, the Judgment Seat of Christ must take place. That is where all Christians are judged in light of the work they have accomplished on earth for Christ. Second, the Marriage Supper of the Lamb must take place. If we are not raptured to be with the Lord until the end of the Tribulation, these two events cannot take place at the time Scripture seems to indicate they will.

> *In church history the period of great missionary outreach, from 1750 until around 1925, was exemplified by the Church of Philadelphia. This was the era of Hudson Taylor, John Wesley, George Whitefield, Charles Haddon Spurgeon, D.L. Moody, and many more. The Salvation Army was founded; a whole galaxy of home missionary agencies sprung up. It was a time of great spiritual awakening.*
>
> *David Jeremiah*
> **Escape the Coming Night**

He Promises to Come Quickly

The last promise Christ makes to the church is, "Behold, I am coming quickly!" He admonishes the church to hold on to their faith that no one may take the crown that is waiting for them. The New Jerusalem is their destination if they will persevere and not give up their loyalty to the Lord.

THE DIRECTION FOR US

Perhaps every church today has representatives of all the Revelation churches in it. Hopefully there are more Philadelphia-type Christians than any other—people who love the Lord and want to serve God. Where there are Philadelphian Christians you will find those things for which the members of that church were commended.

First, you'll find people excited about the open door of ministry, people excited about the future of their church. That's how I feel about my church, and I hope it is how you feel about yours. There is no church that has a greater future than ours—and I hope you believe no church has a greater future than yours! Next, you'll find people who recognize how much God is doing in their church in spite of their "little strength." It is when we feel totally inadequate to carry out the ministry God has given that we are in the right place. Our little strength is made big by Him. Big opportunity and little strength is God's recipe for victory and a great future. Finally, you'll find a church that is teaching the Word of God faithfully week after week at all levels of the church's life. And you will find leaders and members who are faithful to the name of Christ. They serve no other master but Jesus.

But all of those commendable traits will be unprofitable unless we walk through the door God has opened for us. I pray that your church and mine will not only see the open door, but will walk through it on the way to minister in His name.

APPLICATION

1. Record your insights about "brotherly love" from the following New Testament verses.

   a. Romans 12:10

   b. 1 Thessalonians 4:9

   c. Hebrews 13:1

   d. 1 Peter 1:22

   e. 1 Peter 3:8

   f. 1 Peter 1:7

2. Read 2 Corinthians 12:7-10 where Paul describes his experience with having little strength.

   a. How was Paul made weak? (verse 7)

   b. Who was the source of his weakness? (verse 7)

   c. What was the purpose of his weakness? (verse 7a)

   d. What normal response did Paul have to his weakness? (verse 8)

   e. What was God's response to Paul? What was His plan for making Paul strong? (verse 9)

f. What was Paul's response when he understood God's plan? (verses 9b-10a)

g. What was the correlation between Paul's weakness and his strength? (verse 10b)

h. How does Paul's attitude run counter to the prevailing cultural notions about strength and weakness?

3. What weakness do you feel you have in which Christ could manifest His strength?

a. What open doors for ministry do you see before you? What has been your response to those open doors?

b. What does it mean when we fail to walk through a door that Christ opens for us?

SPEAKING OF THE FUTURE . . .

If you have ever tried to put a jigsaw puzzle together, you know that the box top is the template for success. Having a picture of the finished product allows you to see where the various pieces fit together. Bible prophecy is like the top of a puzzle box, and here are five "pieces" of life that fit together better when we see the big picture of what God is doing in the world:

1. Hope for the future. Prophecy tells us Christ comes to rule and reign forever.

2. Confidence in the present. When you don't fear tomorrow, you can have confidence today. People's hearts are failing them for fear because they don't know God's prophetic story.

3. Holiness in living. Christ's appearing is strong motivation for us to keep ourselves pure. What child is not on his best behavior, knowing his parent will soon be home?

4. Evangelism. The chaos in today's world leads many to despair and hopelessness. Prophecy is good news for those who think all the news is bad.

5. Edification, exhortation, and encouragement. The apostle Paul said that prophecy can build us up, set us straight, and keep us going (1 Corinthians 14:3).

Life is not a puzzle to those who know the big picture.

> BUT HE WHO PROPHESIES SPEAKS EDIFICATION
> AND EXHORTATION AND COMFORT TO MEN.
> —Paul in 1 Corinthians 14:3

THE DISGUSTING CHURCH: LAODICEA

Revelation 3:14-22

In this lesson we meet a church that had closed the door in the face of her Lord.

You will find more in-depth information on this lesson in the book *Escape the Coming Night,* chapter 5, pages 75-81.

OUTLINE

Some things happen so slowly we don't recognize the changes. The last of the seven churches to receive a letter from Christ epitomizes a church that has lived without Christ so long they haven't even noticed His absence. He stands at the door knocking to be allowed back in.

I. **The Diagnosis of the Church**
   A. The Laodicean Church is a Compromising Church
   B. The Laodicean Church is a Conceited Church
   C. The Laodicean Church is a Christless Church

II. **The Counsel to the Last Age Church**
   A. Prescription Number One: For Spiritual Compromise
   B. Prescription Number Two: For Spiritual Poverty
   C. Prescription Number Three: For Spiritual Nakedness
   D. Prescription Number Four: For Spiritual Blindness
   E. Prescription Number Five: For Their Christlessness

A s I have traveled in and out of many churches over the years I have noticed how adult Sunday school classes are given Biblical names: the Bereans, the Ephesians, the Timotheans, and so on. But in all my travels, I have never heard of a Sunday school class called the Laodiceans—and for good reason. The church at Laodicea was the saddest of the seven churches addressed by Christ. It was a lukewarm, indifferent church. It is interesting that in His letters to the churches Christ was angered by apostasy, but He got sick at indifference: "I will vomit you out of My mouth" (3:16).

Laodicea was one of a triad of cities consisting of itself, Colosse, and Hierapolis. All three of these cities are mentioned by Paul in the closing verses of Colossians (4:12). There was apparently a close affiliation between the churches in these three cities. Under Roman rule, Laodicea had become a wealthy city, primarily from producing woolen cloth. In church history, Laodicea represents the last period in history before the Lord comes, which makes this letter of Christ so very interesting to us who are alive today and who believe the signs of the Lord's return are evident everywhere.

THE DIAGNOSIS OF THE CHURCH

What should we expect from a church at the end of the age? Unfortunately, compromise is the first characteristic.

The Laodicean Church Is a Compromising Church (3:15-16)

The heart of man is described three different ways in the New Testament. The disciples on the Emmaus road had a burning heart (Luke 24:32), and Matthew 24:12 speaks of a cold heart. But in the Laodicean church was found a different kind of heart, "lukewarm . . . neither cold nor hot." This was a reference to the water situation in Laodicea. There were hot mineral water springs in nearby Hierapolis and cold water springs in Colosse, and there were pipes and aqueducts built to transport the water from both places to Laodicea. But by the time the water got to Laodicea, the hot mineral water had cooled down and the cool spring water had warmed up, so all they got was water that was neither hot nor cold but lukewarm—highly distasteful to drink.

What was it about the Laodicean Christians that made them as distasteful to Christ as lukewarm mineral water is to humans? A lukewarm Christian has compromised his faith. He is no longer fervent in spirit (Romans 12:11) or prayer (Colossians 4:12). He is afraid to take a stand on anything, afraid to offend anyone. The leaders rule by consensus according to what will please the most influential people in the church. There are unfortunately many Laodicean churches in Christendom today. A church that tries to please people and the world will find itself displeasing to God. Lukewarmness is like the woman who prayed for years for her husband's salvation. He finally was saved at a revival and joined the church. When he told his wife of his salvation, she rejoiced. When he told her he joined an evangelistic, Bible-teaching church, she didn't rejoice: "I didn't want you to get that saved!" For her, becoming a Christian meant middle-of-the-road, respectable religion, definitely not commitment. What the world calls zeal and fanaticism the Bible calls commitment to Christ. I remember running into a pastor friend whom I hadn't seen in several years, and his concern over the churches in his particular denomination. He said, "We've lost our zeal. We've lost our sense of urgency. We used to be great soul-winning churches, but we have lost it. We used to be out in our buses trying to get kids to come to Sunday school, but we have put that aside. We've become more respectable, and we've lost our zeal, and something has gone out of our ministry."

While the church has lost its zeal for soul-winning and taking a stand on spiritual and moral issues, we have increased our zeal for entertainment and media and other things. Not that those are bad, but they aren't nearly as offensive to the world. In fact, our efforts have been mainly to duplicate what the world does. We have become lukewarm about the things that got our Savior crucified by a world that knew exactly where He stood by what He said and did.

The Laodicean Church Is a Conceited Church (3:17)

The church at Smyrna thought it was poor when in fact it was rich (Revelation 2:9). The Laodiceans were just the opposite—they thought they were rich when in fact they were "wretched, miserable, poor, blind, and naked." Laodicea was a wealthy banking center and perhaps some of that air of materialistic pride of the marketplace had crept into the church. Somehow their values had gotten all askew.

> *The Laodicean church was a halfhearted church. Perhaps none of the seven letters is more appropriate to the twentieth-century church than this. It describes vividly the respectable, sentimental, nominal, skin-deep religiosity which is so widespread among us today. Our Christianity is flabby and anemic. We appear to have taken a lukewarm bath of religion.*
>
> *John Stott*

David Wilkerson, the author of *The Cross and the Switchblade*, had some powerful insights on the Laodicean mentality found in the modern church:

"Jesus clearly warned that a church would evolve in the last days of civilization which would boast that it was rich, growing, increasing in numbers, and self-sufficient. In other words, a church with great influence, gaining in visibility, and power, while refusing all correction or scrutiny. Jesus said of this church, 'Thou sayest, I am rich and increased with goods and have need of nothing.' How sad that this particular church, arrogant and boastful, is being heralded by so many undiscerning Christians as the glorious last-days church of power and dominion which will subdue the world and bring King Jesus back. It is the Laodicean lie!

". . . I have heard pastors of large churches boast, 'I am going to build the biggest church in America because numbers mean power and influence, and we must have a church big and powerful enough to enforce morality and the will of God in our nation and our communities.' These pastors are that blatant and that boastful. This proud, rich, arrogant church now covets power, not the power of God, but political power. It covets the White House, Congress, and the Supreme Court. Since we have failed to bring about a Jonah-like revival of repentance and a change in the hearts of men, we will according to some, take over the reins of government and legislate righteousness.

". . . God is not at all impressed with this church's bloated estimate of itself. The lukewarm Laodicean church is not destined to dominion, power and authority of any kind. It is destined to judgment. For nearly 2,000 years the church of Jesus Christ has been rejected and persecuted by the world. The blood of millions of rejected martyrs cries out from the ground. For centuries, Spirit-led men and women of God have been burned at the stake, sawn asunder, chased and hunted down like animals. Godly saints were beheaded; others were drowned; many were thrown to the lions. The Bible says they all died in faith and the world was not worthy of them. Am I now to believe that Jesus has changed His mind and has decided to close out the ages with a lukewarm, rich, pampered, boastful, self-centered church? Will the last army of God consist of precinct workers getting out the vote? Will the soul-winners be replaced with petitioners going into the highways and hedges seeking signatures for some social cause?

"Jesus rips off the facade and exposes the truth about the Laodicean church. It is not what it thinks it is. It is not what it says it is. It is not rich, it is poor. It is not on the increase. It is wretched and is about to be forever cut off. It is not strong and in need of nothing. Rather it is naked and shameful. It is not a church with new revelation and deep Scriptural insights. Jesus said it is blind. It is not going to be the vehicle of Christ's dominion on earth, but rather the object of His wrath and abhorrence." [1]

David Wilkerson's words were on target when he wrote them 15 years ago, and unfortunately are still accurate today—if not more so. The power of the Gospel is not found in the voting booth or the size of our churches or the depth of our financial resources. It is found in the power of the Spirit who dwells in those who are committed wholeheartedly to Jesus.

The Laodicean Church Is a Christless Church (3:20)

Christ is standing at the door of the Laodicean church knocking, desiring to be invited in. How sad to think of Him returning to His church at the end of the age and finding Himself shut out! He wants to come in and dine with the church. The Greek word for "dine" refers to the last meal of the day before the dawning of a new day. There is some reason to believe from Scripture that a revival may take place in the last days, but if it doesn't it won't be because Jesus wasn't willing for there to be one. He is standing at the door and knocking. He Himself asked while He was here, "When the Son of Man comes, will He really find faith on the earth?" (Luke 18:8).

In light of Christ's diagnosis of the Laodicean church, counsel is needed. It is too late for them, but not too late for us who live in the Laodicean age of the church.

THE COUNSEL TO THE LAST AGE CHURCH

In light of their lukewarmness, Christ says, "I counsel you" (3:18). Laodicea was a sick church in need of divine prescriptions.

Prescription Number One: For Spiritual Compromise (3:19)

For spiritual compromise Jesus prescribed repentance and zeal: ". . . be zealous and repent." Just as the churches of Ephesus (2:5) and Sardis (3:3) needed to repent, so Laodicea needs to do the same thing.

Prescription Number Two: For Spiritual Poverty (3:18)

Though they think they are rich already, Christ offers them His gold which has been refined in the fire of suffering. If they will come to Him He will make them truly rich, give them something to trust in beyond their material wealth. They needed to move from the gold standard to the God standard. Only Jesus' gold has true value.

Prescription Number Three:
For Spiritual Nakedness (3:18)

Another thing Jesus prescribes for them are the white garments of righteousness to clothe them spiritually. What they thought were the splendid garments that money could buy were really transparent, revealing the shame of their spiritual nakedness. In Revelation 19:8 we discover that the church will one day be clothed in "fine linen, clean and bright," indicating the imputation of Christ's righteousness to us. But we can walk in that righteousness today by being clothed with Christ as we walk in this world.

Prescription Number Four:
For Spiritual Blindness (3:18)

For their blind eyes, spiritual salve was needed. Manufactured in Laodicea was a famous product called "Tephra Phrygia," a pill that, when crushed, was used as an eye salve all over the Roman Empire. They knew how to heal their physical eyes but knew nothing of their spiritual blindness. Their spiritual blindness resulted in all their other conditions. Only when their spiritual eyes were opened would they see their spiritual nakedness and other ailments. Christ's salve could be obtained only by submission to Christ as Lord.

Prescription Number Five: For Their Christlessness

Revelation 3:20 is often used as an invitation verse in evangelism. But it is not written to non-Christians. It is addressed to the end-time church, a church which has shut the door in the face of her Savior. This is beautifully illustrated in the famous picture of Christ, illustrating Revelation 3:20, by the artist Holman Hunt. Many have seen this famous picture, but not all have noticed that the door at

> *The only cure for lukewarmness is the readmission of the excluded Christ. Apostasy must be confronted with His fidelity, looseness with conviction born of His authority, poverty with the fact of His wealth, frost with the mighty fire of His enthusiasm, and death with the life divine that is in His gift. There is no other cure for the loneliness of heaven, for the malady of the world, for the lukewarmness of the Church than the readmitted Christ.*
>
> G. Campbell Morgan

which Christ is standing has no door handle—no way to open the door from the outside. When questioned about this, the artist answered, "It is no mistake. The handle is on the inside. We must open the door."

Have you opened the door to the Lord of the church so that He might give His true riches to you? May the church in the Laodicean age open it wide, unlike her namesake to whom Jesus wrote.

APPLICATION

1. Record the insights you discover from the following passages about fervency in one's walk with the Lord.

   a. Acts 18:25

   b. Romans 12:11

   c. Colossians 4:12

   d. James 5:16

   e. 1 Peter 1:22

   f. 1 Peter 4:8

   How could you apply the concept of "fervent heat" to the spiritual life? (2 Peter 3:10, 12)

   Describe as many different elements as you can from 1 Corinthians 15:58 about what it means to be fervent for the Lord:

2. What was the Apostle Paul's attitude about who we should try to please in the spiritual life? (Galatians 1:10)

   a. If we start compromising by trying to please men, who have we stopped serving? (Galatians 1:10b)

   b. Who did Paul oppose to his face when this person started compromising the truth? (Galatians 2:11)

c. Who was Peter afraid of offending? (Galatians 2:11-12)

d. Who else was influenced by Peter's compromise? (Galatians 1:13)

e. Describe the boldness with which Paul addressed the situation: (Galatians 1:14)

f. How are people like Paul often treated by the church when they take a stand for truth?

g. What will happen if someone doesn't do what Paul did?

h. What had happened to the Galatians? (Galatians 3:1)

i. How was their "spiritual eyesight" similar to the Laodiceans? (Revelation 3:18)

j. How willing are you to be a person who identifies compromise in spite of the condemnation it might bring upon you?

SPEAKING OF THE FUTURE . . .

Suppose you had a visitor coming from a distant state. At what point in his journey would he no longer be far away but near? Would it be when he boarded the airplane? When he was halfway across the country? When he landed in your city? When he walked up the sidewalk? When he rang the doorbell?

Jesus said, "So you also, when you see all these things, know that it is near—at the doors!" (Matthew 24:33). Jesus isn't so very far away. He's already walked up the sidewalk, and he's getting ready to ring the doorbell. His coming is near—at the very door! It's true that every generation of Christians has expected Christ to return in their own era; but it's also true that we're closer to His arrival now than we've ever been before. The Scottish minister, Horatius Bonar, wrote a great hymn that expresses how we should feel about the any-moment return of Christ:

> I know not when the Lord will come,
> Or at what hour He may appear,
> Whether at midnight or at morn,
> Or at what season of the year.
> I only know that He is near,
> And that His voice I soon shall hear.

Christ's return is nearer than it was yesterday, but not as near as it will be tomorrow.

THIS SAME JESUS, WHO WAS TAKEN UP FROM YOU INTO HEAVEN,
WILL SO COME IN LIKE MANNER AS YOU SAW HIM GO INTO HEAVEN.

—Angels in Acts 1:11

Note:

[1] David Wilkerson, "The Laodicean Lie!" *The Evangelist Magazine* (December 1986), 15–17.

THE CHURCH THROUGH THE AGES

Revelation 2:1-3:22

In this lesson we review the seven stages of church history.

You will find more in-depth information on this lesson in the book *Escape the Coming Night,* chapter 5, pages 81-82.

OUTLINE

It's true that we can lose sight of the forest by focusing on the trees. The entire scope of the history of the church was given in seven short visions which John wrote as letters to seven churches. Stepping back and getting the big picture helps us understand where we are today.

I. **The Self-Outline**
   A. The Things Which You Have Seen
   B. The Things Which Are
   C. The Things Which Will Take Place After This

II. **Four Revelations**

III. **Three Views of the Churches**
   A. Practical Application
   B. Perennial Application
   C. Prophetic Application

IV. **Seven Ages, Two Groups**

As we come to the end of our first of four volumes of studies in the Book of Revelation, it is time to recap what we have learned in the first three chapters of the book. There are a number of ways to synthesize Revelation as a whole, and especially the first three chapters. Without further introduction, let's look at the first of four ways to view the prophetic information in this most unique of Bible books, the Self-Outline.

THE SELF-OUTLINE (1:19)

Revelation 1:19 contains a wonderful, three-part outline of the Book of Revelation. In that sense, Revelation is a self-outlined, or self-interpreting, book. So far in our studies we have worked through the first two sections and have only the third (the largest) section to complete.

The Things Which You Have Seen (1:1-20)

The first part of the outline is "Write the things which you have seen." The things which John saw are the things which are written about in the first chapter: The great vision of the glory of Jesus Christ and the powerful description of the Lord Jesus standing in the midst of the candlesticks, observing the churches with His penetrating eyes, seeing the churches for what they really are. When John was on the island of Patmos, he saw Jesus and he described what he had seen in chapter one.

The Things Which Are (2:1-3:22)

The second part of the outline was for John to write "the things which are." So John wrote the seven letters to seven churches of Asia Minor which contained Jesus' evaluation of those churches. "The things which are" were the conditions of the churches at the time John wrote Revelation.

The Things Which Will Take Place After This (4:1-22:21)

The third section begins with chapter four, "write the things which will take place after this." Chapter four picks up after the Church has been raptured from the earth and describes what happens from that point until the glorious appearing of Christ at His Second Coming.

THE FOUR REVELATIONS

Another way the entire Book of Revelation can be summarized is in terms of four different revelations given to John. First, there is the revelation of God (chapter 1). Then comes the revelation of grace extended to the churches (chapters 2-3). Next is the revelation of government (chapters 4-19). And the book concludes with the revelation of glory (chapters 20-21).

THREE VIEWS OF THE CHURCHES

Chapters two and three of Revelation, the section detailing Christ's letters to the seven churches, can be studied at least three different ways: practically, perennially, and prophetically. We have hinted at all three in our studies so far, but will take extended space in this section to elaborate on the prophetic application—that view of the seven churches which should call us to attention regarding our own spiritual posture in the days prior to the return of Christ.

Practical Application

The seven letters to the seven churches were addressed to actual, historically-based groups of Christians in Asia Minor in the first century A.D. They were doing some things right and some things wrong. By way of example, we can gain practical insights into our own spiritual lives by studying their strengths and weaknesses. Once a bright spot in Christendom, modern-day Asia Minor (the country of Turkey) is a dark place spiritually. The mistakes made by the original churches can serve as a warning to us of what can happen if we do not protect our spiritual heritage and leave a legacy for the next generation.

Perennial Application

In between the practical viewpoint (studying the churches in their own historical setting) and the prophetic viewpoint (studying them as representative of seven successive ages of church history) stands the perennial viewpoint. By this we mean that at any time in history there are churches which are like each of the seven churches of Revelation. At any given time in history there

> *In John 14:1-3 Jesus connected His ascension and return—both future events at the time He spoke these words—to His disciples' current experience of peace. He believed that by telling His followers what lay in their future, they would be strengthened to live more vibrantly in the present. Jesus said, in effect, "I've told you about these things so that when they happen, you won't be blown off course. You will have a sense of what God is up to." God intends knowledge of future events to help us "occupy" with a sense of urgency until the Lord returns.*
>
> David Jeremiah
> **Hearing the Master's Voice**

are "Ephesus" churches and "Smyrna" churches and "Pergamos" churches—churches like each of the seven we have studied so far.

And not only are there churches which are like the seven original churches, but there are individual Christians who are like them as well. Some Christians have lost their first love like the church at Ephesus. Some are being persecuted like the church at Smyrna. And some believers have an open door of ministry like the church at Philadelphia. So churches as well as individuals, at any time in history, can learn from the seven churches of Revelation.

Prophetic Application

Perhaps the most profound application of the lessons from the seven churches is the prophetic application. From our perspective in history we can look back from the first century to the present and see the entire ebb and flow of church history. From the church at Ephesus (first century) to the church at Laodicea (the present-day church) we get a panoramic view of the development of the Christian church.

Following are the seven stages represented by the seven churches, and the key phrase from Revelation describing each church and each subsequent phase of church history:

1. Stage One: "You have fallen."

   The period of history represented by the church at Ephesus covers A.D. 33 to 100, that is, the post-apostolic church. The phrase "you are fallen" is indicative of the theological error which crept into the church immediately following the ministry of the apostles. Even the church at Ephesus, to which Paul wrote the beautiful letter of Ephesians, had lost their heart of love for Jesus. Galatians and Colossians were both written to, in part, deal with theological heresy that had raised its head in the churches even while the Apostle Paul was still alive. Second Thessalonians dealt with error regarding the return of Christ. In some way, almost all the letters of the New Testament deal with restoring truth in the churches to which they were addressed.

2. Stage Two: "Tribulation ten days."

   The period of the church at Smyrna covers A.D. 100 to 300. The "tribulation ten days" probably referred to the ten waves of persecution which swept over the church during that 200 year period, beginning with Emperor Nero and ending with Emperor Diocletian. During that time the soil of the Roman Empire was soaked with the blood of the church as many, many Christians gave their lives as martyrs for Christ. The last of the 10 waves of persecution itself lasted 10 long years.

3. Stage Three: "The doctrine of Balaam."

You remember from Lesson 7 the story of Balaam, the Old Testament prophet. He was hired by the king of Moab to curse Israel but blessed Israel instead. Since he couldn't curse Israel, he gave the king another idea: Entice the men of Israel to sin with the women of Moab, and God will destroy Israel in judgment. And that is exactly what the king did, and the men of Israel fell into sin with the women of Moab.

Something similar happened to the church during the Pergamos era, from A.D. 300 to 500. After Diocletian came Emperor Constantine who became a professing, nominal Christian. Christianity was made the state religion of Rome, united in an unholy union of church and state. Pagan temples became Christian churches, and Christian worship and practice became tainted with the pagan practices of the secular Roman Empire. It was the doctrine of Balaam all over again where the people of God were enticed by the glitter of the Roman world, the union of good with evil.

4. Stage Four: "That woman Jezebel."

The fourth period of church history is the Thyatira period which ran from A.D. 500 to 1500. We got to know Jezebel in Lesson 8, and discovered how she brought her pagan, adulterous heritage into the very throne room of Israel when she became the wife of the weak and worldly Israelite king, Ahab. She became the power behind the throne and relentlessly persecuted the people and prophets of God. The union of church with Rome in the previous period initiated a thousand year period of time in which the institutionalized, politicized version of the "church," headquartered in Rome, wreaked havoc throughout the Mediterranean world and Europe. They were indeed the dark ages, the time of the Inquisition when "heretics," such as Martin Luther, the father of the Protestant Reformation (begun in 1517), were persecuted for their beliefs.

5. Stage Five: "A name . . . but dead."

The fifth period is represented by Sardis, and is a period of 200 years—A.D. 1500 to 1700. When conditions in the church under papal authority from Rome became unbearable, Martin Luther initiated a Reformation in 1517. When he was doing penance in Rome as a monk, he supposedly had the insight that "the just shall live by faith" (Romans 1:17) and left Rome and Catholicism forever. While there were changes in Europe, state churches became almost as dominant as the Roman church had been. But at least the Scriptures were unshackled and justification by faith rather than by penance (works) became the watchword of the protesting (Protestant) church.

Toward the end of this period, Rome staged a Counter-Reformation attempting to regain its lost ground, and spiritual stagnation began again. The Protestant church had a difficult time breaking free from the ritualism it inherited from Rome. The church had a name but little life.

6. Stage Six: "An open door."

From A. D. 1700 to A.D. 1900, another 200 year period of time represented the church at Philadelphia. This 200 year period was an explosive period of revival and missionary expansion, originating primarily in England and the United States. It was the age of preachers like Whitefield, the Wesley brothers, Spurgeon, Moody, Finney and others. Social ills such as slavery, drunkenness, child labor, orphans, and poverty were addressed. Missionaries answered the call and headed to the four corners of the world: Carey to India, Taylor to China, Livingstone to Africa, Judson to Burma, Payton to the New Hebrides. God opened the door, and the church went through it in many ways and in many directions.

7. Stage Seven: "Lukewarm."

This is the age in which we live today, the period beginning in 1900 and lasting until the Rapture of the Church—the age of Laodicea, the lukewarm church. It is a sickly church, wretched, blind and naked, torn by cults, kept off-balance by offbeat theologies, and too weak to work at remedying the world's ills. It is a church which has lived in the world while failing not to be of the world at the same time. It is a church consumed with itself and its own comfort while millions march toward a Christless eternity.

No one can see the Prophetic application of the history of the church better than we can, looking back over 2,000 years of history. It is stunning to see how accurately the words given to

> *When the Bible tells us that our Lord will come "as a thief in the night," it is making the point that we don't know when that time is. It is unannounced, unscheduled, and unexpected.*
>
> *When we try to bull our way into mysteries held in the heart of almighty God, we enter into domains where we do not belong. I seem to have my hands full dealing with the past and the present. I'm willing to let the Lord handle the future. No one knows the date of the Lord's return . . . we need to be ready at all times.*
>
> *David Jeremiah*
> **Hearing the Master's Voice**

John at the end of the first century have been so literally fulfilled in the two millennia after he wrote them.

Seven Ages, Two Groups

We prepare now to study the remaining chapters of Revelation where we will encounter seven seals, seven vials, and seven bowls. Each group of seven is separated into two sub-groups of four and three. In each case, the four are successive—they follow each other one after the other. The threes, however, are not successive. Rather they are overlapping, or contemporaneous. And we can see that the seven periods of church history can be viewed the same way.

Group One: Successive

The first four periods of church history followed one after another: Ephesus (post-apostolic) was followed by Smyrna (persecution) which was followed by Pergamos (Rome) which was followed by Thyatira (Dark Ages). But the three following ages did not succeed one another in the same way.

Group Two: Contemporaneous

For instance, when the door for ministry was opened in the Philadelphia period, the previous Sardis period, the dead church, did not end. We still have the Roman church today and churches bogged down in deadness and apathy. And when the expansion of the church began, the Reformation period did not end—its effects continue today. And today, in the Laodicean period, we still have effects from previous periods going on all around us as well, though the Laodicean characteristics are dominant.

Our challenge is to recognize that the Lord could come today (2:5, 16; 3:3, 11, 20). We must hold fast to the truth and to our testimony for Him. We are living, in my opinion, on the bottom edge of the last page of the calendar of history. May God give you and me grace to be found looking heavenward daily as we anticipate being called to meet Him in the air.

APPLICATION

1. As a means of review, describe what is covered in each of the three major sections of the book of Revelation.

   a. "The things which you have seen"

   b. "The things which are"

   c. "The things which will take place after this"

2. Draw a line connecting each church with its primary characteristic:

   a. Ephesus (2:5)   "A name . . . but . . . dead"

   b. Smyrna (2:10)   "The doctrine of Balaam"

   c. Pergamos (2:14)   "An open door"

   d. Thyatira (2:20)   "Tribulation ten days"

   e. Sardis (3:1)   "You are lukewarm"

   f. Philadelphia (3:8)   "That woman Jezebel"

   g. Laodicea (3:16)   "You have fallen"

3. With what spiritual condition and church do you most identify— and why?

SPEAKING OF THE FUTURE . . .

When the Pilgrims on the Mayflower pulled alongside Plymouth Rock in 1620, what if William Bradford had delivered a speech predicting the future? What if he had predicted the thirteen colonies, the American Revolution, the Civil War, the two world wars, and the atomic age?

Impossible? Yes, but when we read the Bible, we see it filled with prophecy about the future of the Jewish people, the coming of the Messiah, and the epochs of human history. These predictions are very specific, and many of them have already been fulfilled exactly as written. The rest will be fulfilled in the future according to Isaiah 46:9–10: "I am God, and there is none like Me, declaring the end from the beginning, and from ancient times things that are not yet done, saying, 'My counsel shall stand . . . .'"

If you have occasional twinges of doubt about the reliability of Scripture, take up the subject of biblical prophecy. Study the passages about Christ in the Old Testament, such as Isaiah 53 and Psalm 22. See how clearly God predicted the future, and let your faith rest in His unfailing Word.

BEHOLD, THE FORMER THINGS HAVE COME TO PASS.
—Isaiah in Isaiah 42:9

Turning Point
Resources
by Dr. David Jeremiah

Escape the Coming Night

How easy it is to dismiss the modern-day prophets who predict the end of the world. But then consider recent examples of world turmoil or the latest evidence of modern decadence, and silently wonder: Is this it? Is this a sign? Is this the end? Dr. Jeremiah offers a fresh, biblically sound explanation of the signs, symbols, prophecies, and warnings of the end times. *Escape the Coming Night* is a penetrating look at the prophetic time machine that is in the book of Revelation and a vivid reminder of how, in the face of coming darkness, we should live today.

Soft Cover Book REVBK *(Can - $20/UK - £8.50)*   **$13**

Study Guides

     Volume 1 REVSG1 *(Can - $14/UK - £6)*   **$9**
     Volume 2 REVSG2 *(Can - $14/UK - £6)*   **$9**
     Volume 3 REVSG3 *(Can - $14/UK - £6)*   **$9**
     Volume 4 REVSG4 *(Can - $14/UK - £6)*   **$9**
     4 Study Guide Package REVSGP *(Can - $44/UK - £18)*   **$28***

Cassette Albums

     Volume 1 REVAL1 (12 tapes) *(Can - $95/UK - £39)*   **$60**
     Volume 2 REVAL2 (12 tapes) *(Can - $95/UK - £39)*   **$60**
     Volume 3 REVAL3 (10 tapes) *(Can - $79/UK - £33)*   **$50**
     Volume 4 REVAL4 (9 tapes) *(Can - $71/UK - £30)*   **$45**
     4 Album Cassette Package REVALP *(Can - $270/UK - £112)*   **$172***

Compact Disc Albums

     Volume 1 REVAL1CD (12 CDs) *(Can - $132/UK - £55)*   **$84**
     Volume 2 REVAL2CD (12 CDs) *(Can - $132/UK - £55)*   **$84**
     Volume 3 REVAL3CD (10 CDs) *(Can - $110/UK - £46)*   **$70**
     Volume 4 REVAL4CD (9 CDs) *(Can - $99/UK - £41)*   **$63**
     4 Album CD Package REVALPCD *(Can - $375/UK - £157)*   **$240***

A 20% Discounted Price

ORDER 1-800-947-1993

Turning Point
Resources
by Dr. David Jeremiah

Jesus' Final Warning

The future did not trouble Jesus, nor was He preoccupied with what might happen. The Gospels make it clear that Jesus, more than any other who walked this planet, knew what the future held. Discover the peace that comes when one understands "Jesus' Final Warning."

Soft Cover Book UICBK
(Can - $20/UK - £8.50) $13
Study Guide JFWSG
(Can - $14/UK - £6) $9
Cassette Album JFWAL (10 tapes)
(Can - $79/UK - £33) $50
Compact Disc Album JFWAL (10 CDs)
(Can - $110/UK - £46) $70

Prophetic Turning Points

Dr. Jeremiah Answers Your Questions about Bible Prophecy

Prophetic Turning Points is essential reading for a world on the brink of its final days. In this easy-to-read question and answer format, Dr. Jeremiah presents answers to some of the most puzzling and often debated questions about Bible prophecy.

Learn from questions such as:

- What is the difference between the Rapture and the second coming of Christ?
- Will Christians have to go through the Tribulation?
- Who is the Antichrist?
- What is the purpose of Armageddon?
- How can I apply prophecy to my life today?

Handbook PTPBL *(Can - $10.25/UK - £4.25)*   **$6.50**

Signs of the Second Coming

Do you have questions about the Second Coming? When will these things be? Jesus replied with the longest answer to any question ever put to Him. Read about the meaning behind Jesus' words, made clear to all believers.

No Study Guide is available.

Cassette Album SSCAL (12 tapes)
(Can - $95/UK - £39) $60
Compact Disc Album SSCAL (12 CDs)
(Can - $132/UK - £55) $84

ORDER 1-800-947-1993

Turning Point Resources

STUDY GUIDES

All Study Guides are regularly priced at $9
An audiocassette or CD album is also available for each of the following series.
(Sold separately. Individually priced.)

Acts: The Church in Action (Volume 1)
Authentic Christian Life, The
 (1 Corinthians, 3 Volumes)
Blessings and Behavior of the Believer, The
 (Ephesians, 2 Volumes)
Celebrate His Love (Christmas)
Christians Have Stress Too
Christ's Death and Resurrection
Escape the Coming Night
 (Revelation, 4 Volumes)
Facing the Giants in Your Life
Family Factor
For Such a Time as This (Esther)
Fruit of the Spirit, The (Galatians)
Gifts from God (Parenting)
Giving to God
God, I Need Some Answers (Psalms)
God in You (The Holy Spirit)
God Meant It for Good (Joseph, 2 Volumes)
Grace of Giving, The (Stewardship)
Greatest Stories Ever Told, The (Parables)
Handwriting on the Wall (Daniel, 3 Volumes)
Heroes of the Faith (Hebrews)
Home Improvement
How to Be Happy According to Jesus
 (The Beatitudes)
How to Live According to Jesus
 (The Sermon on the Mount, 2 Volumes)
Invasion of Other Gods (New Age)
Investing for Eternity
Issues of the Home and Family
Jesus' Final Warning (Prophecy)

Knowing the God You Worship
Learning to Live by Faith (Abraham,
 2 Volumes)
Living by Faith (Romans, 6 Volumes)
Living in the Light (1 John)
Looking for the Savior (Thessalonians,
 2 Volumes)
Miracles of Christ, The
My Heart's Desire (Worship)
Nation in Crisis, A (Joshua, 2 Volumes)
New Spirituality, The (New Age)
Overcoming Loneliness
People God Uses, The
People Who Met Jesus
Power of Encouragement, The
Power of Love, The
Powerful Principles from Proverbs
Prayer—The Great Adventure
Runaway Prophet—Jonah, The
Ruth, Romance, and Redemption
Searching for Heaven on Earth (Ecclesiastes)
Seeking Wisdom—Finding Gold
Signs of the Second Coming
Spiritual Warfare
Stewardship Is Lordship
Tender Warrior, The (David, 2 Volumes)
Turning Toward Integrity (James)
Turning Toward Joy (Philippians)
What the Bible Says About Angels
When Wisdom Turns to Foolishness (Solomon)
When Your World Falls Apart (Psalms)

BOOKS

Escape the Coming Night (Revelation) $13
Gifts from God (Parenting) $19
God in You (The Holy Spirit) $19
Handwriting on the Wall, The (Daniel) $12
Life Wide Open (Purposeful Living) $19
My Heart's Desire (Worship) $19
Power of Encouragement, The $13
Prayer—The Great Adventure $13
Prayer Matrix, The $10
Sanctuary (Daily Devotional) $14

Searching for Heaven on Earth (Ecclesiastes) $22
Secret of the Light, The $15
Slaying the Giants in Your Life $13
Stories of Hope from a Bend in the Road $13
Things That Matter, The $10
Turning Toward Integrity (James) $10
Turning Toward Joy (Philippians) $10
Until I Come (Prophecy) $13
What the Bible Says About Angels $13
When Your World Falls Apart (Psalms) $13

BOOKLETS

Creative Family Living: 20 Ideas for Christian
 Family Interaction $6.50
Family Turning Points $6.50
Financial Turning Points $6.50
How to Encourage Your Children $2.50
Living Right! 25 Behaviors of a Christian $6.50
Patriotic Turning Points $6.50
Plan for Whosoever, A $2.50

Prayer for Whosoever, A $2.50
Prophetic Turning Points $6.50
Signs at the Bend in the Road $2.50
Tour of Duty $4.00
Walking Down the Romans Road $2.50
Who I Am in Christ $2.50
Your Greatest Turning Point $2.50

POSTAGE AND HANDLING CHART	
For orders	Add
Up to $5.99	$1.50
$6.00-$19.99	$2.50
$20.00-$50.99	$3.50
$51.00-$99.99	$6.00
$100.00 & over	$9.00

If you would like a complete catalog
of resources available from
Turning Point, please call
1-800-947-1993 or write
Turning Point ~ P.O. Box 3838 ~
San Diego, CA 92163-1838.
You can also visit Turning Point at
www.turningpointonline.org